Called
to be
His People

Called
to be
His People

by
Glen V. Wiberg

Covenant Press, Chicago

CONTENTS

INTRODUCTION

Confirmation studies have been a vital part of the educational ministry of the Covenant Church from its earliest years. The value of this kind of instruction of the youth of our church cannot be measured, but there can be no doubt that it has contributed substantially to the spiritual life and growth of our people and of our churches. That interest in this kind of instruction continues at a high level holds great promise for the future of the church, to say nothing of what it will do for the youth whose confirmation instruction will be based on this book, *Called to be His People*, and its companion volume, *The Story of the People of God*.

As in the past, the preparation of new confirmation materials has been a joint project of the Boards of Christian Education and Publication, under whose direction a committee of pastors and educators was appointed to determine what type of materials would best serve the needs of the Covenant Church at this point and to select writers for the desired materials. The men chosen for this important assignment were the Rev. Glen V. Wiberg and Dr. F. Burton Nelson, with Pastor Wiberg carrying responsibility for this volume on the Christian Faith and Dr. Nelson for the volume on the story of the Bible and the history of the church.

Recognition should be given to the members of the committee for their excellent work and their devotion to a task which has involved frequent meetings and numerous special assignments over the past four years. Those who have served on the committee are G. Harold Ahlberg, Arthur W. Anderson, Carl Philip Anderson, Glenn P. Anderson, Milton B. Engebretson, James R. Hawkinson, Stanley R. Henderson, J. Robert Hjelm, Al H. Johnson, Ronald F. Lagerstrom, Aaron Markuson (chairman), Craig W. Nelson, F. Burton Nelson, Elmer Ost, and Glen V. Wiberg. Another person who has made a valuable contribution to the production of this volume is Miss Mary Helfrich, who has handled design and layout as well as the selection of illustrative material.

The Covenant Church has a tradition of reading and study which these new materials seek to preserve. We commend them to our churches with genuine appreciation of the dedicated efforts of the committee and the authors and with a prayer for the kind of use that will build faith in all who use them and strengthen the church of Jesus Christ.

AARON B. MARKUSON
CARL PHILIP ANDERSON

Chicago, Illinois
June, 1970

O Church of God Triumphant

O Church of God triumphant above the world's dark fears:
Wherein our souls find refuge through all these earthly
    years;
Christ's steadfast holy purpose, illumined by the cross,
Guards us from evil's power, revealing it but dross.

On Christmas eve her carols have set our hearts aglow,
Her bells on Easter morning with faith still overflow;
Before her hallowed altars we pledge our love in youth,
While in her sacred portals our minds have found God's
    truth.

Her task on earth unfinished till threats of war shall cease,
Her voice must raise a protest where greed still robs men's
    peace;
One brotherhood Christ called for, of ev'ry class and race,
The Church must live the vision that shone in Jesus' face.

O Church of God triumphant we offer now in prayer
Our youth, our fuller manhood, for Christ's great cause to
    dare,
That His redeeming purpose may prove beyond defeat,
Till in the Life Immortal with joy His children meet. Amen.

—The Hymnal

Unit 1
The Church and You

1

Who Am I?

Discovering Who I Am

Sunday	*Psalm 8* What Is Man?
Monday	*Genesis 1:26–28* You—Like Him!
Tuesday	*Ecclesiastes 3:1–15* God's Gifts to Man
Wednesday	*Deuteronomy 7:6–9* Chosen by God
Thursday	*John 1:35–42* You Are—You Shall Be
Friday	*1 John 4:9, 10* The Almighty Cares
Saturday	*1 John 3:1–3* God's Children Now

IN A BEGINNING CLASS of confirmation students, the first assignment the pastor gave was to have each student tell why he had enrolled in the class. Here are some of the reasons they gave:

—I was told by my parents that I had to come
—I am curious
—I want to learn what the Bible means in the twentieth century
—I think I will learn more about the church and what each part of the worship service is all about
—I decided I might as well get in the groove as soon as possible
—I would like to know why God made the earth and what it all means
—I want to see how Jesus works for us and everybody
—I want to become a member of the church
—I think I should get to know God better and through him to know myself better

Perhaps now that you are beginning your second year of confirmation you would like to sharpen your focus and ask again what it's all about. The longer I think about it, the more I am inclined to see in the last statement a reason that is not only big enough for being in confirmation but one that includes all the others and encompasses a lifetime of search and discovery.

The great Danish writer Sören Kierkegaard tells the story of a sensitive young man who, because of a great sorrow in his life, went into hiding. In a letter to an older friend he writes:

> Where am I? Who am I? How came I here? What is this thing called the world? What does this world mean? Who is it that has lured me into the thing, and now leaves me there? Who am I? How did I come into the world? Why was I not consulted, why not made acquainted with its manners and customs but was thrust into the ranks as though I had been bought of a "soul-seller"? How did I obtain an interest in this big enterprise they call reality?

Why should I have an interest in it? Is it not a voluntary concern? And if I am to be compelled to take part in it, where is the director? I should like to make a remark to him. Is there no director? Whither should I turn with my complaint? [1]

Have you ever felt like that young man? Do you ever ask: Who am I, anyway? If you tried to tell someone who you are, where would you begin?

You Have a Name

You would most likely begin with your name. You write it a dozen or more times each day on letters, papers, and application forms. If your name happens to be Mary Smith or Bill Johnson, you know you are only one of a score of people with the same name. But you know also there is really only one Bill Johnson and only one Mary Smith. No one has a signature just like yours. It's something that belongs only to you and no one else.

You Belong to a Family

You would then probably continue by telling who your family is. When you were born, you were linked with a particular family. Not even plastic surgery can remove your family traits. No amount of brainwashing, whether TV advertising or political propaganda, can wipe out the intelligence your parents gave you. Throughout your entire life you will bear the marks of your family by your

    name
    color
    looks
    brain-power
    personality traits
    mannerisms

---

[1] *Repetition*, trans. Walter Lowrie (Princeton, New Jersey, Princeton University Press, 1941), p. 114.

When your parents ask the name of a new friend you have made and what family he's from—whether Ken Anderson's or Reggie Thomas'—it's not because they are being nosey or distrustful but because they identify your friend in terms of a certain family background.

You Have an Address

Next you would most likely tell where you live, where you attend school, who your friends and schoolmates are, and the things that interest you. The answers to these questions would probably begin to show that your life is tied in with many other people. No matter how hard you might try, you know you can't live completely by yourself. Nor would you want to. In the words of a modern song-writer:

> . . . people who need people
> Are the luckiest people in the world.
> We're children needing other children
> And yet, letting our grown up pride
> Hide all the need inside,
> Acting more like children, than children.[2]

This actually says a lot about who you are. You are an individual who belongs to a group of people. You depend on others, and they depend on you. If by some freakish accident you were to be pulled out of this interwoven network of people and stranded like Robinson Crusoe on some desert island where you would be forced to live out your life in total isolation, you would be something less than a full human being. And yet the wonder of it all is this: You are different from everybody else. You have your own ideas about things, your own ways of doing things, and your own feelings. All of this says that you are yourself, too.

---

[2] "People" from the musical *Funny Girl,* copyright by Bob Merrill and Jule Styne.

Your First Assignment

But what else would you say in letting someone know who you are? Stop your reading right now and take your first assignment for the year. Write at the top of the first page of your notebook: WHO AM I? Then tell briefly whatever you need to tell in order to describe the real you.

Well, how did it go? Are you satisfied with your answer? You probably discovered it wasn't such an easy question after all. Maybe it takes a lot more thinking. This is so because you may have a lot of experiences to sort out, feeings to understand, doubts and anxieties to resolve. Yet to find out who you are and what you are becoming is one of your central drives as a human being. I hope that during this second year of confirmation this study will help you to fill out in greater detail the first page of your notebook. For it is really about you—who you are, where you came from, and why you are here.

The Good News: God Loves You

Your Bible, *The Hymnal,* your textbook, your pastor and church are eager to spell out for you the Good News. (Did you know that is what the word "gospel" means?)

The first thing you need to understand is that in all the many ways in which you describe yourself, in all your many belongings to family, friends, schoolmates, neighbors, and the ever-expanding circle of town, city, state, nation, and world, you are special, so much so that God is calling you to be one of his People.

This final stage of confirmation is to help you add to your "Who am I?" page something that sounds like this:

> I am one whom God loves. He not only made the world, and loves the world, but he made and loves me. He does this not because I happen to have good looks, or brains, or because I behave so well that he can't help loving me. But he loves me because he is God and "God is love." Long before I knew him, he loved me.

In other words, we can respond to the young man who was running away, or to the person who just can't figure things out, by saying: "There is a 'director' to whom you can make your remarks, to whom you can turn with your complaints. And he is concerned about you." So, you see, knowing yourself as one of his people is a very personal thing—just as personal as your

    signature
    family
    friendships
    clothes
    music
    hair-do

And just as personal as saying "I love you" or "I believe."

The Good News: The Church Cares about You Too

But the Good News is something more:

Just as God places you in a family, a neighborhood, a school, so he places you in a church—in a congregation just like yours—in order to help you to know yourself, not simply as someone special but as one whom God seeks to be part of his Servant-People.

In other words, this part of the book is about you and your belonging to God's People, the church. It is to help you look at yourself at this important time of your life by encouraging you to listen to the One who is calling you into the fellowship of believers and then by assisting you to give a sincere and intelligent answer to this question:

Am I ready to become a member of God's People? Am I prepared to let this belonging shape what I think and feel, hope, and do, so that the real "me" comes through loud and clear?

Beginning the Search

Even in facing a question like that, it's re-assuring to know that we don't start from scratch. Most likely the church has been present already in your life in one way or another. You have been taught about God since you were very young. You have learned some hymns and prayers. You have come to feel at home in God's house. And now for the past year you have been studying the story of God's People through the ages. You have gathered up certain facts and bits of information in the process. This is good!

But now as you move toward the home-stretch, the time has come when you must move beyond mere facts. Until now you have accepted things simply because your parents or other adults said so. Now it's time for you to get into the conversation yourself. You can do this by learning to think in fresh ways about what and in whom you believe; where and to what you belong. Don't be afraid to ask questions or to let your mind soar. To discover who you are means to assert your independence and to begin to search on your own. After all, how will you really get to know who you are if someone else has it all figured out for you?

I promise you that this part of your study will not be so much a "let me tell you" affair as it will be a jumping-off place for your own thoughts. At best, I hope this study will hold out a friendly hand to you from one who is still a pilgrim. But let's begin where you are and join other pilgrims who know themselves as those whom God loves and calls to become his People.

Prayer

Heavenly Father, for all the forces and persons that have made me what I am I give you now my deepest thanks: for just being born, for a home I didn't build, a family I didn't create, food I didn't grow, furniture I didn't make, possessions I didn't earn, freedom I didn't fight for, medicine I didn't produce, laws I didn't think up, protection I didn't provide.

But I also thank you that because I exist I can cause things to happen. I know how I see things and how I feel about them and that there are some things I can choose and decide. Grant that what I already am may be shaped by what I would like to be. Give me the courage to discover the one person I can be, the one person you want me to become. I offer this prayer in the name of One whose business it is to make the most of people like me. Amen.

Some Things To Do

1. Be prepared to share with your class how you have begun to describe yourself. Why not do this by making a collage of yourself?

2. Look at current TV programs and movies, listen to pop records, or find poetry or novels and report on what you think they are saying about man. How does this square with what the Bible says? If you have records or poetry, bring them with you to class so you can share them.

3. Discuss how advertising tends to define who you are. What's true about it? Where does it go wrong? Illustrate by specific examples.

4. Choose either of the following and put into your own words what you think is meant:

   a. In the first chapter of his *Institutes of the Christian Religion,* John Calvin said:

   Nearly all the wisdom we possess consists of two parts: the knowledge of God and of ourselves . . . . And the proper order requires us to discuss God first and then proceed to treat ourselves . . . . since no man ever achieves a clear knowledge of himself unless he has first looked upon God's face and then descends from contemplating Him to scrutinize himself.

   b. There is an old Jewish folk tale about Rabbi Zusya, who, toward the end of his days, worried about the accounting he would be called upon to give in the after-life. "It is that you have not been a Moses throughout your lifetime that troubles you?" asked his friends. "No," he replied, "my concern is that I was not Zusya."

5. Discuss in small groups one or more of the following questions, then report back to the class:

a. If you are a unique person, what does this say about your freedom and responsibility to decide how you dress, talk, and act?

b. To what extent do you have a right to decide for yourself without considering what other people think?

c. Do you think you can belong to groups that might threaten to destroy the freedom to be yourself?

d. What do you think of the right of the "hippies" to be "hippies"?

e. Do people in your community respect the uniqueness of people who are "different"?

MEMORY WORK

What is the highest and most important knowledge?

The highest and most important knowledge is to know God and his son, Jesus Christ.

"And this is eternal life, that they know thee the only true God, and Jesus Christ whom thou hast sent" (*John 17:3*).

The Nativity panel from the Christ Window,
Wesley United Methodist Church,
the Church of the Wesley Foundation
at the University of Illinois, Urbana

2

What Is the Church?

Word-pictures of the Church

Sunday	*1 Corinthians 12:12–13* Like a Body
Monday	*Ephesians 2:19–22* Like a Building
Tuesday	*John 15:1–8* Like a Vine and Branches
Wednesday	*John 10:11–16* Like Shepherd and Sheep
Thursday	*Philippians 3:20–21* Like a Colony
Friday	*James 1:16–18* Like a Harvest
Saturday	*Revelation 21:1–4* Like a Bride

REPORTER: Good evening, ladies and gentlemen. This is your TBS roving reporter, Walter Scoopmore, bringing you another TBS special report. Tonight we are presenting a documentary on "The Church Today: USA." For this program we have selected a cross-section of American churchgoers to express what they understand the church to be, what its purpose is, and where it seems to be going. We take you now to Chicago, Illinois, where we interviewed a teen-ager who felt strongly about . . .

Click!

Let's not change channels or turn the TV set off because you don't "dig" a program like this. But let's stop here because it's your question now. What do you understand the church to be? Before you read any farther, write your answer on the second page of your notebook. Put it down as honestly as you can—even if it doesn't happen to be what adults would say or what they might want you to say. Remember, you are a partner in this conversation.

Several Opinions

One group of young people expressed its opinions in a word-association game using the word "church" and came up with the following terms:

building
worship
Sunday
people
boring
conservative
sermons
suppers
feelings
squabblings
preacher

Do any of these words appear in your answer? Which ones? Remember that just as there is no single answer to the question WHO AM I?, so there is no one answer to this question about the church.

Not too many years ago I felt a little like Diogenes,[1] who carried a lantern and went around asking, "How can I find an honest man?" I was looking for an honest and complete answer to the question: What is the church? Then I realized that I was not alone in this search. In fact, I discovered that this question is being asked all over the world. The sharpest minds among scholars and churchmen have been wrestling with it. Though they have not been able to summarize their findings and views into a definition that will satisfy all Christians, they are working at it. And we can too!

One reason for our difficulty with the question is that many of us have never taken the time to consider it—seriously, I mean. The church has simply been around, and we have taken it for granted. For most of us, it has been a place where we have been wanted. But then we have had those moments when we have wondered just how, where, or if we really belonged.

An Outside View of the Church

We can shed some light on the question if we try stretching our imaginations a bit. Just for the fun of it, imagine that a visitor from another planet suddenly arrives in your community. After the initial excitement of his appearance wears off and he has had time to become adjusted to a totally different planet, what would such a visitor from outer space conclude from his first encounter with the Christian church? How would you help him understand what the church is? How would you distinguish it from other organizations like Junior Achievement, Future Farmers of America, Boy Scouts, PTA, or a hundred other similar groups?

---

[1] A Greek philosopher

You would probably begin by pointing out certain things which indicate the presence of a church. You might remind him that those pointed structures rising above the elms and maples of your community which he saw as he was looking for a suitable landing place for his spaceship were church buildings. Sometimes they can be identified by an object called a "cross," but not necessarily so. You would have to point out that the church may also be found in less conspicuous buildings—empty stores or even homes.

Buildings by themselves, however, would tell your visitor from outer space very little. After all, by comparison with skyscrapers, factories, places of business and finance, centers of communication, recreation, and entertainment, the buildings that house churches might seem rather unimpressive. You would have to encourage him to find his way to one of these buildings on a Sunday morning and ask him to observe what's going on.

Take your church, for example. What might he observe that would give him some clue as to what the church is? He might be struck first of all by how different things are in the church compared to other things in American life. After all, in the rest of society people attach great importance to having the latest gadget, being up to date, and following the newest styles in everything. But in the church he would find a curious reversal. He would see people listening to readings from a very old book which tells about events and persons of long ago. He would hear people singing hymns and saying prayers as though they were talking to someone who, so far as he could see, was not there. He would see a man get up and speak for nearly thirty minutes. He would also observe certain actions in which some or all of the group participated: distinctive acts like washing with water (Baptism), or sharing a simple meal (Lord's Supper)—acts, he would be told, that have been performed for nearly two thousand years.

But then he might have some questions: What draws these people together? What happens here that makes it worth their time? Does anything happen?

He might be perplexed when you tell him that in the United States six persons out of every ten belong to organizations called churches. And he will probably be thrown into total confusion when you inform him that among all these churches there is no one single organization or way of doing things; rather, there are at least 256 different ways of doing things through organizations called "denominations" to which the churches belong. Then he might ask: But is there anything that combines or unites all of these different groups?

An Inside View of the Church

Now you are on the spot. You will probably send out an SOS for your pastor. Then, again, you may have an answer ready. But it's just here where your visitor from outer space would either tune in or tune out. It may be where you yourself either stay with the church or become a "drop-out." Here the shape of the real answer must begin to form. You would have to say to your visitor that the church cannot be seen or known at all from the outside as buildings, ways of worship, or different organizations.

A People with Memories

You might say something like this:

> To know what the church is you have to know it from within, on the inside. You have to share its memories . . .

Let's pause a moment and take that last phrase in slow motion. What binds all these different people, customs, and organizations together is a shared memory. The people who make up the church remember what God did in the history of Israel and in the story of Jesus Christ. This ancient story has become their story. When you gather for worship next time, notice these tangible signs of remembered things we share in common:

—the Bible opened before the congregation, the book containing the record of God's mighty acts . . .

—the cross as a visual reminder of the death of Jesus for us and our salvation . . .

—the table where the Lord's Supper is celebrated, usually inscribed with the words "This do in remembrance of me"

A People with Hope

You might go on to say:

To know the church from within, you have to accept its ideals of righteousness and love, and dream its dreams . . .

Step inside the door on any Sunday morning, and you sense how tentative everything is. You often hear it in the hymns and prayers—a longing to be on the way, like an old fishing boat tugging at its moorings when the tide goes out. You discover that all Christians look forward to something yet to come. You might call it a desire for a better world, a looking forward with hope.

A People Who Care

Then you would also have to say:

To know the church from within, you have to care about the church and what it stands for.

Put simply, this means: You have to listen to its word about Jesus Christ, feel sorry over the church's failures— and also your own—and set your feet moving in a new direction. When you begin to care about the church, you become part of a community that shapes life, that influences what you think, how you feel and act, what you consider important, why you are here, and where you are going. In other words, the church can be—if you will let it

—the major force shaping the one life you have to live. It can help you forge for yourself some central meanings and direction. It can help you find the real you.

I don't know what the TBS roving reporter discovered in the documentary: "The Church Today: USA." But maybe now you are ready to tune-in and listen to the descriptions of the church God has given us in the Scriptures. Listen to how Paul puts it:

> "So you are no longer outsiders or aliens, but fellow citizens with every other Christian—you belong now to the household of God" (Ephesians 2:19, Phillips).

Or listen to Peter's first letter:

> "But you are a chosen race, a royal priesthood, a holy nation, God's own people, that you may declare the wonderful deeds of him who called you out of darkness into his marvelous light. Once you were no people but now you are God's people; once you had not received mercy but now you have received mercy" (1 Peter 2:9, 10).

Knowing yourself in some such way as that provides a base on which you can build a whole life.

Prayer

> O God our Father, we praise you for calling us to be your servant people, and for gathering us into the body of Christ. Grant that, together, we may live in your Spirit and so love each other that we may have among us the mind which was in Christ Jesus our Lord, to whom be all honor and glory, forever. Amen.
>   —The Book of Common Worship

> O merciful God, bless this particular church in which I live. Make it, and all the members of it, sound in faith, and holy in life, that they may serve you, and you bless them; through Jesus Christ our Lord. Amen.
>   —William Laud, Archbishop of
>   Canterbury in the 17th century

Some Things To Do

1. Look up in a concordance (your pastor or church library has one) and see how often the phrase "people of God" appears. What does this mean to you? Do you think it could make you a more dynamic person? Would it help you feel closer to other Christians in your community?

2. Describe the various meanings of the word "church." Discuss in class.

3. List all the word pictures you can find in the New Testament describing the church. Don't be afraid to ask for help if you need it.

4. List the denominations given in your local telephone directory under "churches."

5. In *A Book of Worship for Covenant Churches* there is "An Order for the Reception of New Members" which begins with the pastor addressing the congregation like this:

   "Dear friends, the church is the body of Christ, the dwelling place of the Holy Spirit. It is the household of God and the fellowship of believers in Christ Jesus."

   Translate this in your own words so that it makes sense to you or conveys to a total stranger to the church what it's all about.

6. Discuss with your parents how people can know or understand themselves as God's people. Share your findings with the class.

MEMORY WORK

What is the church?

The church is the whole company of those who, confessing Jesus Christ as Savior and Lord, are united in fellowship with God and with one another.

"So then you are no longer strangers and sojourners, but you are fellow citizens with the saints and members of the household of God, built upon the foundation of the apostles and prophets, Christ Jesus himself being the cornerstone" (*Ephesians 2:19, 20*).

First "Mission Friends" church, Swede Bend, Iowa, and "The New Song" North Park Covenant Church, Chicago.
Photos by Varde

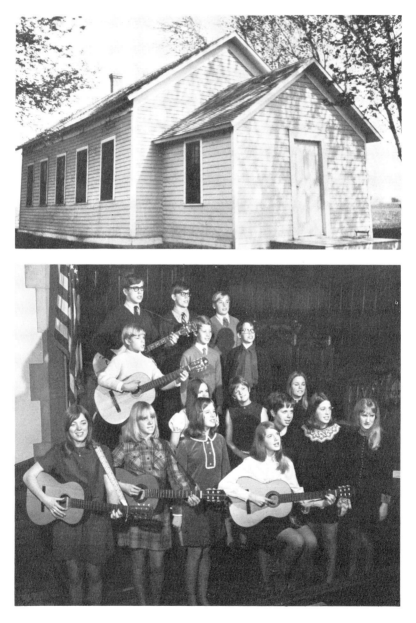

3

The Miracle
of the Church

Kindled by Fire

"THE CHURCH—a miracle? That sounds almost like double talk. It looks like anything but a miracle!" Granted. There are plenty of things that seem to deny it. I can almost guess what you're thinking. You would probably argue your case like this:

Point 1: Worship is usually dull and boring. The prayers, music, and sermons seldom "turn me on."

Point 2: Beliefs are obscure, hard to understand. I hear words like "redemption" and "atonement" and never quite know what they mean.

Point 3: The church doesn't seem to be doing too much about the real problems that "bug" me and the world I live in.

Point 4: The church is filled with a lot of phonies, people who preach better than they practice.

Point 5, 6, 7: And so forth.

I admit that at times it hardly looks like a miracle. But let me remind you of one thing: the miracle of the church is often hidden. You have to go looking for it. If you don't, you might miss it. This, of course, doesn't mean that the church is never boring, obscure, ineffective, or hypocritical. But it is simply to say there is some evidence that points to the presence of something else at work in its life.

The Miracle: An Unbroken History

One question which Communists keep asking young Christians in East Germany is: "Why haven't you died out yet?" The theory is that if Communism changes the face of society, removing all the injustices which exist in it by establishing a classless society, then the church, which is seen to be the guardian of the status quo—things as they are—will automatically disappear. "We've done all this," they say, "but you Christians are still around. Why? Explain to us why you don't die out."

That's a good question: Perhaps you can find the answer by asking another: How did my congregation begin? Where did these people I see every week get their faith? There *is* a mysterious quality about the church, something you begin to discover when you consider its long history. Some strange things have happened in the past to make it what it is and to give it—with all its failures—this survival quality that refuses to die out.

One Congregation in Particular

Let's take a Covenant congregation which has a history that might be somewhat similar to that of your own church. Later on you might want to do some research on your own that would tell the story of your congregation. On the cornerstone of our church building the date 1952 is inscribed. Something important happened then. A casual observer might conclude: "This church dates from 1952." But he would be wrong. It goes back much farther than this.

Anniversary booklets tell me that my congregation was organized on June 26, 1886, in a small hall located on East Federal Street in Youngstown, Ohio. Twelve charter members met in the glow of an oil lamp to bind themselves, as they put it, "in sacred covenant to give the Scandinavian people the gospel in their native tongue, to administer the Sacraments according to the Word of God, to take up Sunday school work, to extend aid to the poor and sick in the community, and to extend the gospel to the heathen in foreign countries. . . ." So you might conclude that my congretation dates back to 1886. Wrong again!

You would have to go one step farther back to 1881. In the spring of that year seven Swedish immigrants gathered in the home of Gust Nelson on East Front Street to hear the Word of God. Who were these seven people? You would have to know something about where they came from and something about the "spark" that brought them together. A miracle, perhaps? These seven people came from Sweden, where things were happening. There God was busy trying to wake up his sleepy church. He was also busy shaking men loose from their old habits and sins and making them new men. These seven people who came from Sweden to America in search of a better life economically had also been moved by the stirrings of new life God was bringing to his people. As we reflect on this we see that what brought them together was bound up with several factors:

—19th-century Sweden with its difficult working conditions but with its stirrings of new life
—a longing to hear the Word of God
—a desire to share the new life with other believers
—the very human need to find a place of refuge against the loneliness of struggling for a foothold in the strange new world.

But not even the 19th century provides the real starting point of this congregation. From here on, your study of the story of God's people will furnish you with the rest of the facts. The outline takes us back in history like this:

—Back to the 16th century, the Protestant Reformation, and the Lutheran Church of Sweden
—Back to the time before the Reformation, when there were only two main branches of Christianity: Western and Eastern. (Your church and mine has its roots in the Western branch.)
—Back to the 11th century, when Eastern Christians and Western Christians were still united
—Back another thousand years to the first century of the Christian era and the beginning of the church's struggle against the Roman Empire
—Back a few more decades until you come to what has sometimes been called "the birthday of the church," the Day of Pentecost
—Back to the life, teachings, death, and resurrection of Jesus
—Back to the history of the Jewish people

So the church building with a cornerstone that says 1952 is quite misleading. It has, in fact, a history much longer than the United States or any other nation in the world. And even when the church seems at times to be on the verge of dying out, it has a strange way of coming back—not always in the same way, but in new and more exciting ways that better fit God's plan for his People. Now do you begin to see the miracle? But what keeps it going?

The Miracle: A Gift of the Spirit

Here the words we use in trying to describe the miracle nearly break down. We must talk about "spirit," or, more precisely, about the "Holy Spirit." It begins to sound a bit mysterious. But perhaps it will help you to think for a moment about what happens at a football game. Your team is out there fighting. You are pulling for it for all you're worth. Suddenly there is a breakthrough. Your team scores a touchdown. "Spirit" takes over. You jump up and down. If you were asked to describe exactly why you acted as you did, you would probably have to say: "I don't know what came over me. I just had to yell my head off. It was our team!" You can't put your finger on it, but it was something very real. You became fired up with enthusiasm for your group—call it "team spirit" or "school spirit" or whatever you will.

When we speak about the Spirit as that miracle which keeps the church going, we are not talking about an "it" but about a personal Presence. Here is one way of putting it:

> The Spirit is God alive in our consciousness, full of majesty and power—present in a way unique for each person but present also in a way that transforms individuals into a community, a living fellowship of God's People.

Now read again in Acts 2 the story of one of the strangest moments in religious history. Shortly after the crucifixion and resurrection of Jesus the disciples gathered in a room to celebrate the Jewish Feast of Pentecost, a festival commemorating the giving of the Ten Commandments. Suddenly they heard something that sounded like a hurricane. Then flames of fire seemed to be darting from one to another. They became excited. (Remember the football game?) But the real miracle was not the excitement. It was this:

> They came to a new understanding of themselves as well as of God which enabled them to speak so that even strangers could understand them.

Peter's Sermon: The Good News

Some people on the outside, however, thought they were drunk. Then Peter took hold of the situation and began to explain this new power that had come over them. Here is what his "sidewalk sermon" was about:

> First, what was promised long ago by the prophets was coming true then and there . . .

The prophet Joel prophesied a day when the Spirit would be given to all. This Spirit would cause young men to have visions and old men to have dreams—that is, the Spirit would help people see things from God's viewpoint, understanding themselves and the world in which they live as his People.

> Second, what was happening was tied up with the Good News of Jesus of Nazareth, who did many mighty works and had been put to death but was brought back to life by God.

When the people heard the Good News, they wanted to know what to do about it. Peter concluded his sermon on this note:

Third, they must repent (that is, change their direction) and be baptized. If they would do this, they would also receive the gift of the Spirit.

Something happened. It's hard to explain. But it gave to these early Christians a new vision, a new power and confidence, that sent them out into the Roman Empire proclaiming the Good News to everyone who would listen.

The Miracle Today

Where is the miracle of the church today? Is it still happening? You go to church, sing, pray, and listen to the sermon, or you reach out a helping hand for some worthwhile cause and nothing seems to happen. But every once in a while it is different. Out of the blue you experience a flash of something or other. It's like a door opening—be it ever so briefly. You catch a glimpse that suddenly makes your everyday world seem new. For an instant, you grasp what life is all about, where you fit in, what you have to do. God's word becomes a personal message to you. He is very much alive for you. And you feel close to others. The miracle has happened!

Of course, you can make a case against the church for seeming to be anything but a miracle. But perhaps if we went to church expecting something to happen, it would. It wouldn't be dull and boring but aflame with God's presence, just as it was when the church was born. We would then see the church as C. S. Lewis [1] describes it, "spread out through all time and space and rooted in eternity, terrible as any army with banners."

---

[1] Philosopher, scholar, and author. One of his most popular books is *The Screwtape Letters,* from which this quotation is taken.

Prayer

Most gracious God, my heavenly Father, in whom alone dwells all fulness of light and wisdom; illuminate my mind by your Holy Spirit, in the true understanding of your word. Give me grace that I may receive it with reverence and true humility. May it lead me to put my whole trust in you alone; and so to serve and honor you that I may glorify your holy name and give encouragement to my neighbors by a good example. Since it has pleased you to number me among your people, O help me to pay you the love and devotion I owe, as your child and servant. I ask this for the sake of my Master and Savior. Amen.

—John Calvin (adapted)

Some Things To Do

1. Make a time-line of the history of your local congregation, using whatever resources are available—anniversary booklets, interviews with older members, and so forth.

2. Write an essay on the Jewish Festival of Pentecost. (You can find help in a Bible dictionary which you can borrow from your church library or pastor). Then be prepared to discuss in class in what sense Pentecost as reported in Acts 2 added something new to the life of the early Christians and what this newness means to us today.

3. Read Acts 2:22–24 and 29–36. List the things in the life of Jesus that Peter refers to in his preaching. If the same things were told in a newspaper article, would we think it was bad news or good news? Why?

4. Discuss with the class whether or not you think Jesus planned for an organized church such as we have today.

5. Think about this: What are some of the signs of the presence of the Holy Spirit in your life? in the life of your congregation?

MEMORY WORK

Who is the Holy Spirit?

The Holy Spirit is God everywhere present and powerful, working in us, in the church, and in the world.

"Now to him who by the power at work within us is able to do far more abundantly than all that we ask or think, to him be glory in the church and in Christ Jesus to all generations, for ever and ever Amen" (*Ephesians 3:20, 21*).

4

Nice People or New Men?

Mysterious as the Wind

Sunday	*John 3:1–15* New Birth
Monday	*Acts 8:26–39* Conversion of an Ethiopian
Tuesday	*Acts 9:1–9* Conversion of Saul
Wednesday	*Acts 10:30–48* Conversion of Cornelius
Thursday	*Acts 16:11–15* Conversion of Lydia
Friday	*Acts 16:19–34* Conversion of the Philippian Jailer
Saturday	*Romans 6:1–11* Death and Resurrection

HAVE YOU EVER HEARD someone say, after being at Bible camp,

> "I became a Christian that evening in our cabin when my counselor prayed with me"?

or this?

> "I met Christ at the campfire service and was saved."

I remember hearing one say in his excitement over his camp experience:

> "I can't wait until next year to be saved all over again."

Maybe you have said something like this yourself. Think for a moment about these statements and what they mean. What's right about them? Or wrong? Or perhaps inaccurate?

A Definite Experience

However these young people may have been straining for words to describe what happened, they were saying something important, something about which the church is deeply concerned—not simply at Bible camp but all the time. Among other things, they were saying that

> —one must come to know God on a person-to-person basis in order to be a Christian
> —life with God must have a beginning

You find this emphasis often in the New Testament. Jesus was always making this point. One day he was talking to a very fine man by the name of Nicodemus. He said something like this: "You know the facts of life. You had an honest-to-goodness birth, or you wouldn't be here.

That's how you arrived. But if you want to be an authentic person, that is, to see life as it is meant to be lived out under God's rule, you have to be born all over again." You can read the story for yourself in John 3.

Or look again at how Peter concluded his sermon at Pentecost:

> "Repent, and be baptized every one of you in the name of Jesus Christ for the forgiveness of your sins; and you shall receive the gift of the Holy Spirit"   (Acts 2:38).

Let's take it slow-motion,

—Repent, that is, change your direction; begin to think some new thoughts; let God's Word be a fire in your minds to set you on a new course.

—Be baptized, that is, accept the sign God gives so that everyone can see you have entered the company of the People of God and have made a new beginning.

—Receive the gift of the Holy Spirit. That is what makes you new and helps you to become a new person who is always growing in life with God and with others.

The story ends like this: "So those who received his word were baptized" (Acts 2:41). We are not too much concerned about which comes first, baptism or faith. What's more important is to know that they belong together. In fact, you can't really know yourself as a member of God's People at all apart from this new way of seeing, thinking, feeling, and acting. You don't just drift with the crowd into the Christian church. You are born into it with the birth from above.

There is an old Negro spiritual that puts it like this:

> My feet looked new,
> My hands looked new,
> The world looked new,
> When I came out the wilderness
> Leaning on the Lord.

A song like this makes us feel that something happens which changes a person from being a spectator to a full participant, from being an "outsider" to being an "insider."

No One Pattern

God seems to throw away the mold every time he makes a person new. He doesn't deal with any two people in exactly the same way. You read the Gospels, and you discover that Jesus called each disciple in his own way: one from the place where he was gathering taxes; others from the seashore where they were tending and repairing their fishing nets; another from a tree, and so on. Jesus put it this way in talking to Nicodemus about the new birth:

> "The wind blows where it wills, and you hear the sound of it, but you do not know whence it comes or whither it goes; so it is with every one who is born of the Spirit" (John 3:8).

In other words, you can't put it into any formula. You can't say when, or how, a person must be reborn. You can't even say that it will appear as a complete turn-about in every instance. No one pattern fits all. For God moves in mysterious ways in people's lives but in ways that are just right for each one.

A Parable

Maybe it's something like falling in love. It happens in many different ways:

> (1) Love at "first sight." Two people discover that they are meant for each other. They fall head over heels in love. They can tell you when and where it happened.
> (2) To others love comes less dramatically. Two people may think they're in love but then discover it was just a case of infatuation or passing fancy. However, after some time of frustration and unhappiness, they start

going together again until love enters their lives to stay.

(3) Then there are those who meet in childhood as family friends. Through the years friendship deepens until at last they discover they are in love.

So it can happen with our experience of God.

Three Examples

(1) There is one group for whom the new birth comes as a sudden, dramatic happening. This is what may have happened with those young people at camp. It often happens that way to people in large evangelistic crusades such as those conducted by Billy Graham. But it can also happen when a person is alone. Perhaps it will happen for you when you are walking home from school or off in the woods. It may happen while you are reading the Bible, listening to music, doing something for someone else, or maybe doing nothing. But you meet the living Christ, and you know you have to say Yes or No to him.

It happened in a sudden, dramatic way for Saul as he was traveling to Damascus on a mission to try to destroy the Christian movement. God used a sudden vision to speak to him. It happened something like that for Augustine when he was walking in his garden—but without any blinding light. Notice how he describes it:

> I sent up sorrowful cries: "How long, how long? Tomorrow, and tomorrow? Why not now? Why is there not this hour an end to my uncleanness?" . . . I was saying these things and was weeping in the most bitter contrition of my heart, when, lo, I heard the voice of a boy or girl, I know not which, coming from a neighboring house, chanting and oft repeating: "Take up and read; take up and read." . . . So . . . I rose up, interpreting it in no other way than as a command to me from heaven to open the book and read the first chapter I should light upon . . . I seized, I opened, and in silence I read . . . "put ye on the Lord Jesus Christ" (Romans 13:13, 14).[1]

---

[1] *According to Thy Word*, p. 216.

(2) There is a second group for whom the new birth has come over a long period of personal struggle with doubts or sins. A person in this group might think he has become a real Christian; at least he wants to do what is right. Then he wakes up to find that he has not yet arrived. Something is lacking. Finally, after years of searching and striving, he finds Christ or is bound by him.

Do you recall how John Wesley described his encounter with God?

Or let's take a more recent account of a man's struggle. C. S. Lewis, a college professor and author, tells his story like this:

> You must picture me alone in that room in Magdalen, night after night, feeling, whenever my mind lifted even for a second from my work, the steady, unrelenting approach of Him whom I so earnestly desired not to meet. That which I greatly feared had at last come upon me. In the Trinity Term of 1929 I gave in, and admitted that God was God, and knelt and prayed; perhaps, that night, the most dejected and reluctant convert in all England. I did not then see what is now the most shining and obvious thing: the Divine humility which will accept a convert even on such terms. But who can duly adore that Love which will open the high gates to a prodigal who is brought in kicking, struggling, resentful, and darting his eyes in every direction for a chance to escape? The words *compelle intrare*, compel them to come in, have been so abused by wicked men that we shudder at them; but properly understood, they plumb the depths of the Divine mercy. The hardness of God is kinder than the softness of men, and His compulsion is our liberation.[2]

(3) Then there is the third group. These are persons who have been brought up in a Christian home and constantly nurtured in the Christian faith. The eyes of their faith have opened like those of a newborn baby, slowly, gradually, until they have seen the full light of day. Their rebirth is almost unconscious. If asked, they perhaps could

---

[2] *Surprised by Joy* by C. S. Lewis, Harcourt, Brace and Company, New York, 1955, pp. 228, 229.

not tell when they were converted. Yet they know it has happened—and continues to happen—as they permit the Good News to enter into their hearts and shape their lives. They are like Paul's good friend and colleague Timothy, who from childhood knew the Scriptures "which are able to instruct you for salvation through faith in Christ Jesus" (2 Timothy 3:15).

Dr. Theodore W. Anderson, the fourth president of the Covenant Church, belongs to this group. He puts it like this:

> Reared in a devout home on a Kansas homestead, as I was, my experience was more like Timothy's. I cannot recall a time when I felt isolated from Christ. I agree with Dr. F. B. Meyer of England that I will have to learn in heaven exactly when I was born again. I do, however, remember a season as a teen-ager when I craved more certainty about my relationship to my Savior. This led me to an earnest searching of the Scriptures and fervent prayer. That resulted in a deeper peace and a fuller commitment to my Lord. Vividly do I remember my first public testimony. It was given in Prayer Week in a little stone church on a hilltop on a Kansas prairie. Throughout the week I felt I should make such a confession but timidly postponed it. In the closing moments of the final service of the week I rose and used the words of Paul, "I know in whom I have believed and am persuaded that He is able to keep that which I have committed unto Him against that day." [3]

So, you see, the most important thing is not *how* the new birth happens but that it *happens*. Whether it comes gradually or suddenly, whether openly or in the secret of one's heart, there must come a moment of saying Yes, of choosing sides, of committing oneself to him who loved us long before we knew him—if we are to know ourselves as his People. However different, we are all alike when we are able to say: "I know I am a child of God. I desire to be led by his Spirit day by day."

---

[3] From a private letter.

A Continuing Life

But the new birth is only the beginning. There must also be a continuing growth. You never have the feeling that you have arrived. You do not become arrogant about your life with God or what you have experienced of his grace. You know you are still on the road. Christians are indeed "people of the way" (Acts 9:2). This means at least two things:

> (1) that they are opening themselves to the Good News, allowing the steady pressure of its message to revise their thinking, to shape and transform their whole life.

Of course, we all have a long way to go. But this is not so strange. Peter, you recall, had trouble with his ego; John with his bad temper; Thomas with his doubt. Yet after some years in the presence of the Lord, they became stones in the foundation of the temple God was building. So with us. Little by little the pagan in us is tamed and shaped after God's likeness—both in the way we think and the way we act toward our neighbor and toward God. It's a sign we are alive!

That Christians are "people of the way" also means:

> (2) that they are letting the Good News turn them outward toward the world.

The new birth is never an end in itself. Rather, like human birth, it means being ushered into a new environment. We can no longer live the warm, sheltered, constricted life of the womb. Nor can we live in some kind of spiritual incubator. We are born to live in the world, to serve God's purpose there. Isn't that exciting? Think of your own life. Your birthright as God's child is that you have come to this moment in history with something only you can give and do, with something that can make a difference in the world. Whatever that is, you can never live a settled life since your feet have been placed on the road which leads to the coming of God's kingdom for all men.

Is this just pious day-dreaming? The church says No. Such things really do happen. There are such new men, whether their names happen to be Paul or Timothy, Augustine or Wesley, C. S. Lewis or T. W. Anderson. You can find them at Bible camp, in confirmation class, in your congregation, in churches everywhere. Such things can happen to us

> —whenever we become discontented with ourselves and begin to wonder: Who am I? Where am I going? What is the meaning of my life? and set about to find the answers
> —whenever we begin opening ourselves to the Good News, believing it, as John Calvin says, "with the heart, not merely with the head"
> —whenever we say Yes to this strange seeking out of us, this powerful calling us by name, this sense of finding out who we are and why we have been created, this struggle to be obedient.

In those whom God is making new, there you also find the true church!

Prayer

> God, I am thankful for what others have known about you.
> But now, it's only you and I.
> There is a lot about this chapter I don't understand.
> But perhaps this uncertainty is your way of inviting me to do some searching on my own and to say Yes right now to what I do understand.
> What gives me hope, dear God, is that when I pray, study, and live before you, I don't need to try to dress up in someone else's clothes and opinions, someone else's doc-

trines and experiences, but you have planned so well in your mercy and by your Spirit that I can find the clothes which are tailored to fit me.

Help me where my faith falls short.

I offer this prayer in the name of Jesus my Savior. Amen.

Some Things To Do

1. Discuss in class: What makes being a "nice" person a dangerous thing?

2. Write an essay on this question: If one of your schoolmates asked you how to become a Christian, what would you answer? (If you use words like "repent" or "believe," be sure you explain what these words mean.)

3. Translate into your own words what you think these statements mean:

   a. "I can never say I am a Christian, only that I am becoming a Christian." (Sören Kierkegaard)

   b. "Before I became a Christian I do not think I fully realized that one's life, after conversion, would inevitably consist in doing most of the same things one had been doing before: one hopes, in a new spirit, but still the same things." (C. S. Lewis)

   c. "It is the mark of a converted man, inasmuch as he is converted, that he can say, 'I am I.'" (Erik Routley)

   d. "The church is not an organization of good people; it is a society of sinners. It is the only organization in human society that takes sinners into its membership just because they are sinners." (Charles Clayton Morrison)

4. Study these five conversion stories in Acts:

Acts 8:26–39	The Ethiopian Eunuch
Acts 9:1–9	Saul
Acts 10:30–48	Cornelius
Acts 16:11–15	Lydia
Acts 16:19–34	The Philippian Jailer

   In what ways are they different? in what ways similar?

5. Toward the end of the year, shortly before you are confirmed, your pastor will have an interview with you about your personal relationship to Christ and the church. Start thinking now about what things in your life have brought you closest to God; who are the people who have helped you most to want to become a Christian; what you have learned in Sunday school through the years; how God has been helping you in confirmation.

6. Plan an interview with an older member of the congregation and also with a younger member (preferably a college student) in which you ask them how they came to know Christ. Your pastor can make suggestions of persons to contact.

MEMORY WORK

What is conversion?

Conversion is that act by which man turns with repentance and faith from sin to God.

"The time is fulfilled, and the kingdom of God is at hand; repent, and believe in the gospel" (*Mark 1:15*).

The Church's One Foundation

The Church's one foundation Is Jesus Christ her Lord;
She is His new creation By water and the word:
From heav'n He came and sought her To be His holy bride;
With His own blood He bought her, And for her life He
    died.

Elect from ev'ry nation, Yet one o'er all the earth,
Her charter of salvation, One Lord, one faith, one birth;
One holy Name she blesses, Partakes one holy food,
And to one hope she presses, With ev'ry grace endued.

'Mid toil and tribulation, And tumult of her war,
She waits the consummation Of peace forevermore;
Till, with the vision glorious, Her longing eyes are blest,
And the great Church victorious Shall be the Church at
    rest.

Yet she on earth hath union With God the Three in One,
And mystic sweet communion With those whose rest is
    won:
O happy ones and holy! Lord, give us grace that we,
Like them, the meek and lowly, On high may dwell with
    Thee. Amen.

—The Hymnal

Unit 2
Where It's Happening

5

The Good News of God

Good Christian Men, Rejoice!

IT'S SUNDAY MORNING AGAIN, and you're in church. The organist begins playing the opening hymn. You come down to earth with a thud and start fumbling in your hymnal. You recognize the tune. You have sung it many times before. Oh, yes, "The Church's One Foundation." By the time you locate the place and stand up with the rest of the people, you find yourself singing the second line:

"She is His new creation by water and the word."

Perhaps because of what you've been studying recently in confirmation those words hit you. You don't sing any further. By the time the hymn ends you have it figured out pretty well. You say to yourself:

"By water"—that must have something to do with baptism. "The Word"—that must have something to do with the Bible from which the pastor reads, and maybe the sermon too.

The riddle is nearly solved, except for those words about "the new creation." You know a few special people who seem more alive than others. But the church? Everything you have come to associate with the church seems pretty old and behind the times. Where is this church I've been singing about all my life? Is it here among these people I know so well, most of whom don't seem to be too different from anyone else? They don't look different. Same clothes. Same language. Same cars. Same houses. Same everything. What's new about them?

The Humanness of the Church

Those of us who believe in the church have to admit that this "new creation" we sing and talk about is not always evident in all the churches, all the time. Churches have a way of concealing at times the real church instead of demonstrating it. Maybe this is only to admit that because it is made up of human beings the church isn't all that Jesus meant it to be. No matter how hard humans try, they're not perfect. Even in the church people are people. But then again the problem may be that we fail to see the living struggle going on in those whose minds and hearts have been touched by God.

If, however, our proposal is an honest one—that we discover who we are, where we are going, what is the meaning of life for the People of God—we must begin to define what such a people really is like. If the church is like many other clubs and organizations in your town, made up of people who also belong to the PTA, Rotary, NAACP, the Future Farmers of America, and so forth, it becomes even more important to ask what makes it different. What are the distinguishing marks of the church?

Several Marks of the Church

Throughout its history the church has done a lot of thinking about this question, not simply as a pastime but because its very existence has depended on it. You see signs of the church's struggle to define itself in the second century, when it came up with this formula:

"The church is where the bishop is."

Later on, in the fourth century, when the church was hammering out its faith, you come across these words in the Nicene Creed:

"I believe in one holy (or catholic) and apostolic church . . ."

This was another way of attempting to describe how the church could be distinguished from other religious or secular groups. Christians still frequently talk about the church in these terms:

The church is one
The church is holy
The church is catholic (universal)
The church is apostolic

During the time of the Reformation, Protestant Christians were accustomed to locating the church by these distinguishing marks:

> "The church is the assembly of saints in which the Gospel is taught purely and the sacraments are administered rightly."   —Augsburg Confession, Article VII

That definition may still prove helpful, especially if we put the accent on hearing, believing, and obeying the gospel.

But let's look again at the first days of the church. There is no better source for the study of the early church than the Book of Acts. Since it was probably written within sixty years of the church's beginning, it provides an invaluable picture of what the early church was like and what was involved in belonging to it. After describing the coming of the Holy Spirit and the sermon of Peter on the Day of Pentecost, Luke goes on to say:

> "So those who received his word were baptized, and there were added that day about three thousand souls. And they devoted themselves to the apostles' teaching and fellowship, to the breaking of bread and the prayers. And fear came upon every soul; and many wonders and signs were done through the apostles. And all who believed were together and had all things in common; and they sold their possessions and goods and distributed them to all, as any had need. And day by day, attending the temple together and breaking bread in their homes, they partook of food with glad and generous hearts, praising God and having favor with all the people. And the Lord added to their number day by day those who were being saved" (Acts 2:41–47).

Notice the marks that distinguished the church in the excitement of those first days:

crowds	wonder and awe
baptism	mutual aid
apostles' leadership	sharing of goods
teaching	confidence of outsiders

fellowship   new members
breaking of bread   joy

Among these several characteristics, there are four things to which the early Christians devoted themselves that seem to have priority in setting the church apart from other groups:

the apostles' teaching
fellowship
breaking of bread and prayers
service of men

Do you see these marks in your congregation? When a congregation really devotes itself faithfully to these activities, you will find the church very much alive and eager to be obedient in all other areas of action where it is called to serve.

The Apostles' Teaching

The apostles occupied a special place of importance in that early community of believers for several good reasons:

—they were eye-witnesses to Jesus' life
—they were the first proclaimers of the Good News of Jesus
—their witness later took shape in the written form of the New Testament

Toward the end of the first century the Apostles' Creed began to appear in a form somewhat similar to the way we have it today. It was called the Apostles' Creed not because the apostles wrote it but because it contained a concise and convenient summary of what the apostles preached and taught concerning God. Thus the apostles had an important role to play in helping the early church to understand its faith. Faithfulness to their message became one of the signs by which one was able in those days to recognize the true church.

The Proclamation

Actually, there were two parts to the message of the apostles. The first part was the preaching. The word for "preaching" in the Greek New Testament is "kerygma" (pronounced keh-roóg-mah). This referred to that part of their message which was addressed primarily to those outside the church. It was missionary preaching.

We have already taken a brief sampling of Peter's sermon on the Day of Pentecost. It was not an argument for the existence of God or a lecture on obeying the law or how to follow the dictates of one's conscience. It was, rather, a story about things that really happened. It was that all Jesus began to do and teach from the beginning (Acts 1:1) was now exploding into life again with meaning and power for every man.

Let's look more closely at this message about Jesus:

> "I speak of Jesus of Nazareth, a man singled out by God and made known to you through miracles, portents, and signs, which God worked among you through him, as you well know. When he had been given up to you, by the deliberate will and plan of God, you used heathen men to crucify and kill him. But God raised him to life again, setting him free from the pangs of death, because it could not be that death should keep him in its grip"
> (Acts 2:22–24, *New English Bible*).

Notice what he says about him:

—Jesus is the "man singled out by God," the one anointed, selected, given the stamp of God's approval
—Jesus is the one made known through mighty deeds of compassion
—Jesus is crucified "by God's deliberate plan"
—Jesus was raised again simply because being the man he was death could not win out over him

This sermon, like the other summaries of early Christian preaching in the Book of Acts, contains only the bare outline of what the apostles said and must not be taken as a complete statement of the Christian faith. But you can begin to feel something of the excitement in their message. They had Good News to speak! In fact, this is what has called the church together.

The Application

The other part of the apostles' message was teaching. The word for "teaching" in the Greek New Testament is "didache" (pronounced dee-dah-kéy). This referred to that part of their message which offered instruction to those who had accepted the Good News. It was concerned with how the preaching could be applied in practical, everyday ways. Take this brief sample of teaching from the New Testament:

> "So then, if you've been given new life in Christ, go after the things of the New Order, in which Christ rules with God's authority." . . . Which means more specifically breaking with certain things like "blowing your top, getting all steamed up, acting ugly, throwing your weight around, running off at the mouth with dirty jokes," etc., and putting in their place such things as "a tender heart, kindness, genuine humility, loyalty, persistence."
> (Colossians 3:1, 8, 12, *Cotton Patch Version*, Jordan)

Is the teaching something dry and musty? Not if we understand that the kerygma (preaching) and didache (teaching) belong together. The teaching grows out of the preaching and seeks to indicate the style of life that follows in those who accept the Good News. Both constitute the message of the apostles and the early church.

Sunday Morning Again

But what, really, is it all about? How is the message of the apostles Good News for you? Imagine you are back in church. Still wondering about the newness you sang about and where it can be seen, you tune in on the pastor's sermon. You hear him saying something like this:

> . . . what God has done in Jesus is to show you and me and everybody else in the world that we count for something. Sometimes we feel we are nobody. We don't know who we are. We feel dead.
>
> But God refuses to let us live in death. He brings the gift of life to us in the midst of death. He does this through the coming of Jesus Christ. He has entered into our world, taking upon himself our frustrations, our broken relationships, our death. He wants more than anything else to help us find out again who we are as People of God.
>
> But it cost something. He became a nobody. He entered into our life of death by accepting death on a cross. But the story does not end there. God entered the tomb of his Son and gave him life again. He couldn't stay dead.
>
> As we die with Christ, letting go of our false dreams, our phoney values, our self-centered egos, so we also rise from the dead to new life. God enters our graves and speaks the word of life. We live again as his Son lives. We know who we are, why we are here. The whisper of our identity we have been seeking and couldn't find now becomes a shout of triumph and joy. "We are God's children now and it does not yet appear what we shall be . . ." It doesn't mean that all the whys and wherefores are solved. It doesn't mean that now we wear halos. But it does mean that we have uncovered the clue to finding out the way in which these lives of ours can become significant. Let us pray . . .

Where can the church be found? This is not the whole answer, but it is at least a beginning:

—wherever the message of the apostles concerning Jesus is being proclaimed and received as Good News

—wherever people are letting this message shape their style of life according to the pattern given in Christ

—wherever peoples' hearts are so full of the Good News that they must share it with others

It's something like the hymn says—"a new creation"—not in any perfect and complete sense but breaking through here and there into the old order of things.

Prayer

Lord, call us into the church.
Call us in often,
and teach us the old words and old songs
with their new meanings.
Lord, give us new words
for the words we wear out.
Give us new songs for those
that have lost their spirit.
Give us new reasons for coming in
and for going out into our streets
and to our homes.
As the house of the Lord
one moved like a tent through the wilderness,
so keep our churches from being rigid.
Make our congregation alive and free.
Give us ideas we never had before,
so that alleluia and gloria and amen
are like the experiences we know in daily living.
Alleluia! O Lord, be praised!
In worship and in work, be praised!
Amen.[1]

---

[1] Herbert Brokering, From *Lord, Be With*, (Concordia Publishing House, St. Louis, Mo., 1969), p. 151. Used by permission.

Some Things To Do

1. Choose one of the following passages that record the preaching of the apostles—Acts 2:14–39; 3:13–26; 4:10–12; 5:30–32; 10:36–43; 13:17–41; or 1 Corinthians 15:1–7—and rewrite it as a story for the front page of your daily newspaper.

2. Write an essay beginning with these words: "The gospel of Jesus Christ is good news to me because . . . ."

3. Report on one of the following:

   a. The origin and growth of the Apostles' Creed. Ask your pastor for a book on church history or on the history of Christian doctrine.

   b. The five marks of the church as discussed in *According to Thy Word*, chapter 22, pp. 396, 397. (Your church library or pastor will have a copy.)

   c. How your church sanctuary represents the Good News —through architecture, building materials, furniture, windows, symbolism, and the colors of the church year (if these are used).

   d. Ways you see your congregation teaching; tell whether you think some of the teaching could be improved and how.

4. Be prepared to discuss the following questions:
   a. In what ways is your church like the church of the first century? In what ways is it different?

   b. In what ways is your church like other groups and organizations in your community? In what ways is it different?

5. Do some role-playing, using the situation of a person who justifies his staying away from church by pointing to the weaknesses and failures of its members. Where would you go from here? (Students will be selected to act out the situation. After the drama has been played and stopped by the leader, each player will discuss how the person he represented must have felt inside. Finally, the group will discuss their feelings while they witnessed the drama.)

MEMORY WORK

What is the gospel?

The gospel is the good news of God's redeeming love for man, made known in the life, death, and resurrection of Jesus Christ and his continuing rule over us.

"For God so loved the world that he gave his only Son, that whoever believes in him should not perish but have eternal life. For God sent the Son into the world, not to condemn the world, but that the world might be saved through him" (*John 3:16, 17*).

6

Sharing
the New Life

All Brothers

Sunday	*Matthew 18:15–20* Gathered in His Name
Monday	*1 Corinthians 12:12 and 13* Baptized into One Body
Tuesday	*Ephesians 2:11–18* The Broken Wall
Wednesday	*Ephesians 4:1–6* Unity of Spirit
Thursday	*Acts 4:32–35* Of One Heart
Friday	*Philemon 1–25* A Beloved Brother
Saturday	*2 Corinthians 8:1–5* Rich in Generosity

KATHY STRUGGLED long and hard over her confirmation assignment. The pastor had asked the class to write their own creed, the things they believed and tried to live by. Among other things she wrote:

> The most important part in being a Christian is having a private, personal relationship with God.

Kathy had expressed something which in terms of her own life was true. She was a real Christian. You could tell it by the way she lived with other kids, how she did her confirmation work, by her faithfulness in attending worship, and by her genuine concern to be helpful wherever she could. In a score of ways, her personal life with God shone through.

She was expressing something about which the church is also very much concerned. (How many times have you heard your pastor speak about the need for a "personal commitment" to Christ?) Without knowing it, Kathy was also on the same wave length as a distinguished American philosopher, Alfred North Whitehead, who said that "religion is what a man does with his solitariness" (that is, his life apart from the crowd).

Christianity—Personal but not Private

But is that all there is to being a Christian? A personal life? Yes! Private? At this point, we would have to ask some further questions.

> (1) How does this personal life with God get started in the first place?

Everyone who has ever become a Christian has become one directly or indirectly because of the witness and presence of the Christian community. If one becomes a Christian through reading the Bible, then one is using the book of the church. For apart from the church's witnessing to God's mighty acts, writing, preserving, and translating the message, there would be no Scriptures. If one becomes a Christian through the preaching of the Good News, that proclamation is being given by a member of the church. Or if one becomes a Christian through the influence of home and parents, that nurture has had its source in the faith and teaching of the church. I can't be a Christian all by myself. Outside and apart from the church I could never know the Christian experience which Kathy called "a personal relationship with God."

We would have to ask another question:

(2) What keeps a personal life with God going?

We suggested earlier that our individual ways of becoming Christians are very different. Even the ways we have of explaining what has happened to us in Jesus Christ are bound to be different. Yet it is something we have together. We meet one another—whether in confirmation, Sunday morning worship, Hi-League, or Bible camp—and in doing so are strengthened and renewed by what we hold in common. Christ often becomes more real and challenging to us in fellowship with others than when we are alone. It's as if the pieces of the jigsaw puzzle suddenly fit together when Christians share what they see and know of Christ. Without some such meeting, such mutual support, we would soon slip backward into our old patterns of thinking and acting and fall by the wayside.

While Christianity is something very personal, it is never private. It is a life shared with others. Perhaps Kathy, like many of us, never bothered to think about how closely her personal life with God is bound up with the faith and life of others.

Is the Church Part of the Good News?

Many historians express something close to amazement over the church of the first century because of the new kind of community it represented. They might put it something like this:

If the church had merely announced a new philosophy or teaching, it would have attracted little attention, and would have been tolerated. But there was something more to the young church besides new ideas. It changed people's relationships. It created a new kind of life together that upset the traditional ways in which men were accustomed to relate to one another.

You recall the many nations and languages represented at the foundation of the church on the Day of Pentecost. This was only the beginning. Before long you discover even greater variations—

Jews and Greeks
Romans and barbarians
slave and free
rich and poor
educated and unschooled
prison guards and members of Caesar's household
young people and aged

—all sharing a new and exciting life. Differences of language, race, culture, class, or occupation no longer mattered. A "new creation" had come into being through Christ. It was not a group of people who all thought alike or who happened to have the same tastes or interests. They didn't even need to like one another particularly. Yet they belonged together. Because they were partakers of Christ, they were partakers of one another. They were all brothers.

The church had Good News. But more, the church *was* Good News. For it was beginning to fulfil in a striking way God's purpose for mankind from the very beginning. The church said to the outsider, the lonely and lost:

In Christ you belong—whoever you are. Here you count for something. You are somebody. You fit in. You have a place.

That Overworked Word "Fellowship"

The Greek word for this new life together is "koinonia" (koy-noh-nee-ah), meaning sharing, having something in common, fellowship. In one of the key passages for our study we read: "And they devoted themselves to the apostles' teaching and fellowship (koinonia)" (Acts 2:42). In the early church it meant a great deal more than the word "fellowship" suggests to us today. We use the word for almost any type of chumminess, like

service clubs   coffee and doughnuts
bridge parties   church suppers
bowling leagues   block parties

In our world of so many human fellowships, it is almost impossible to capture the full impact of the biblical word. But we can try to recover the word by looking at some of the ways it is used and translated in the New Testament:

"The grace of the Lord Jesus Christ and the love of God and the fellowship (koinonia) of the Holy Spirit be with you all" (2 Corinthians 13:14).
"And all who believed were together and had all things in common (koinonia)" (Acts 2:44).
". . . Macedonia and Achaia have been pleased to make some contribution (koinonia) for the poor among the saints at Jerusalem" (Romans 15:26).
"The cup of blessing which we bless, is it not a participation (koinonia) in the blood of Christ?" (1 Corinthians 10:16).

At least two things become clear:

First, koinonia is something God gives and creates, not something we can manufacture. In the church, we don't pick and choose those with whom we have fellowship. Those whom God calls and brings together are given to us as brothers and sisters. We are fed by God as we celebrate this gift of life together in the Lord's Supper.

Second, koinonia is something given to us to demonstrate. It imposes certain obligations. It may mean giving up a certain standard of living for the sake of poorer brothers and sisters in Christ. It may mean giving cold, hard cash in showing practical concern for others. But it always means being bound together by the Spirit in serving the mission of the church.

In the last chapter, you recall, we began to define what a People of God looks like. We asked: What kind of behavior sets the church apart from other groups? Let's ask the question now in terms of the church as koinonia or fellowship.

Freedom and Honesty

First of all, the church as koinonia is characterized by honesty. At its best, the church is found where people are learning to share their questions, problems, insights, and faith with one another in freedom and honesty, without being afraid. You will most likely find this in small groups which meet to study the Bible or to discuss a book or some current event or situation in the community.

Where there is a real sharing in grappling with honest-to-goodness problems, you find a people beginning to level with each other. Such honesty is bound to expose people's differences. Christians *do* see things differently. But it's just at the point of disagreement that koinonia is given. It provides a way of dealing with differences, removing obstacles, and tearing down walls of hostility that keep people apart, afraid, suspicious. (Read what Paul says about this in Ephesians 2:14–16.)

Here's how one young person found it.

Ralph, who was 16, attended his first church business meeting. It had been a rough session. Important issues were at stake. There was a rapid cross-fire between certain people. Some strong words were spoken. Disillusioned by this experience, Ralph said to his pastor on leaving: "Boy, I wouldn't have your job for anything!" After a few weeks Ralph came to talk things over with his pastor. His first words were: "I came to tell you I want to prepare for the ministry." He told the rest of the story. "You see, it began that night of the business meeting. The next Sunday I saw these same people who had differed so strongly worship together. They greeted one another without any hard feelings whatever and without holding any grudges. If that is what the church is, I want to serve it."

He had discovered the fellowship. People could be honest in their differences. They could say what they thought. But they could do this because they knew the power of love, forbearance, and forgiveness in dealing with their differences.

Mutual Care

The church as koinonia is also characterized by mutual care for one another. Someone who knew human nature very well remarked that we are never totally sorry to hear of another's bad luck; we congratulate ourselves secretly that it did not happen to us. Similarly, we are never totally glad over another's success; we are always just a little bit jealous. That's human nature. But in the church, if it's really the church, when one person is hurt, everybody hurts. If one person makes a mistake, there is always someone who understands. We are a body. If I have a toothache, I don't feel good anywhere. So with this body, the pain of one is the pain of all, even as the joy of one is the joy of all.

Openness to All Men

Finally, the church is a fellowship that is characterized by its openness to all men. The first major struggle of the early church had to do with accepting non-Jews into membership. Did a person have to become a Jew before accepting Jesus? The answer was an emphatic No! The church had been called by its Lord to be a genuinely open fellowship, open to men of every nation, color, and class, and closed only to the man who does not accept Jesus as Savior and Lord.

The church that practices or supports segregation is a contradiction of the Good News. On the other hand, where different kinds of people are being drawn together in one body, you can see before your very eyes that the Good News is at work. The world, too, can see the miracle of the life together that God desires for all men. The church's business is not only to be this kind of open fellowship but to extend it to everyone. Where this is happening, you find the church really being the church.

Listen to how the New Testament describes it:

> "There is neither Jew nor Greek, there is neither slave nor free, there is neither male nor female; for you are all one in Christ Jesus" (Galatians 3:28).
> "For by one Spirit we were all baptized into one body—Jews or Greeks, slaves or free, and all were made to drink of one Spirit" (1 Corinthians 12:13).

What the church really has to offer is

—not just a friendly handshake
—not just a place to meet the right people
—not just coffee and doughnuts in the church basement
—not a pep talk on how to win friends

but life bound together by one Spirit in love and service to one Lord. Good News? I have a hunch Kathy would agree.

Where the church does not live up to its gift of koinonia and demonstrate it, it is called to repentance!

Prayer

I've searched for community in many places, Jesus.

I was often looking in the wrong places, but I don't think my motive was altogether wrong. I was looking futilely and hopelessly there for fellowship, belonging, and acceptance.

Now, in this moment, which many people would label "loneliness," or "nothingness," I want to thank you, Jesus. In this moment—in this place and with these other persons—I have found community where and as it is. It seems to me it is your gift.

I am here with these others for only a few hours. I will be gone tomorrow. But I won't be searching so desperately any more. I know I must accept community where you offer it to me. I accept it in this moment. Thank you, Jesus.

—Malcolm Boyd [1]

Some Things To Do

1. Read Acts 9:1–31, Acts 10:1–48, or the Letter to Philemon. Write a short story or a play showing how the principal characters acted in representing the fellowship (koinonia) and the effects of their actions.

2. Make a study of your congregation.

   a. How does your congregation attempt to demonstrate its practical care for its own members? What does your pastor do? Is there a program of visitation to the sick and shut-in? Are there ways in which you can be of assistance?

---

[1] *Are You Running With Me, Jesus?* by Malcolm Boyd. Holt, Rinehart and Winston, Inc., 1965. p. 43.

b. What does your congregation do to welcome visitors? Do they find your church friendly or indifferent? Are there ways members can learn to know visitors? Is there anything your class can do?

c. Does your congregation have a program to reach people who live in the neighborhood where the church is located? Do these people come to the church? How would they be made to feel welcome?

d. Does your congregation include people of different types? Do you think people of great differences could find a real sense of belonging in your congregation? What, if anything, do you think could be done to see that this happens?

e. Is your congregation open to people of different races? Would they be made to feel at home if they applied for membership? Does your church have a sense of mission to people of other races?

f. How does your congregation share in fellowship with the churches of other denominations in your community and beyond? What contacts does your denomination have with other Christian bodies? Are these contacts being encouraged or discouraged by your local congregation? Why?

3. Think about the following statement. Be prepared to (a) tell in your own words what the author is saying and (b) give an illustration of the idea.

Therefore the real children of God have peace among themselves, something that is so highly necessary that without it everything is but a sham, and we, with all our zeal for the kingdom of God, disgrace the gospel of peace and bring condemnation upon ourselves. But peace within the group does not mean that all think alike, each wishing to see, as it were, his own self in another, but it does mean that each one recognizes his own brother in Christ, whatever else the condition may be. It is not the identity in thought and comprehension of all possible particulars that constitutes that perfect bond by which we love one another; that bond, rather, is the mutual filial condition to which we are born from above.[2]

---

[2] C. J. Nyvall, *Travel Memories*, (Covenant Press, 1959), pp. 20–21.

4. Discuss in class whether it is possible to live the Christian life apart from the worship and fellowship of the church. You may wish to do so by reacting to this statement:

   . . . we have been discovering anew that the Church is not an appendage to the Gospel; it is itself a part of the Gospel. The Gospel cannot be separated from that new people of God in which its nature is to be made manifest. (Stephen Neill)

5. Make a collage or poster from newspapers and magazines, showing those forces in society which split people apart and those forces which bring people together.

6. Plan a project in which your class or Hi-Leage might make a practical demonstration of koinonia.

MEMORY WORK

What is the purpose of the church?

The purpose of the church is to celebrate new life in Christ, build up one another in the Christian faith, proclaim the gospel to all men, and be his servants in the world. These are the duties of the members of a church.

"You are a chosen race, a royal priesthood, a holy nation, God's own people, that you may declare the wonderful deeds of him who called you out of darkness into his marvelous light. Once you were no people but now you are God's people; once you had not received mercy but now you have received mercy" (*1 Peter 2:9, 10*).

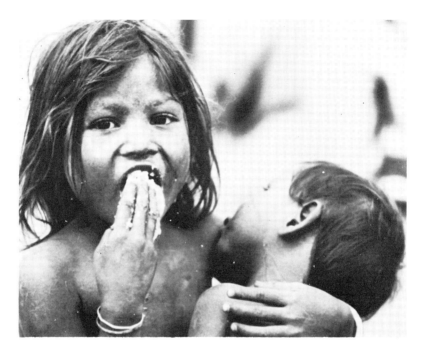

Food sent by CARE to ease famine in India.
Photo courtesy of Religious News Service

7

Breaking Bread

Bread for the Hungry

Sunday	*Exodus 16:2–15* Bread from Heaven
Monday	*John 6:1–14* The Miracle of Loaves
Tuesday	*Mark 14:17–25* The Last Supper
Wednesday	*Luke 24:28–35* The Risen Christ Appears
Thursday	*Acts 20:7–12* On the First Day
Friday	*1 Corinthians 11:20–34* Wait for One Another
Saturday	*Isaiah 58:6–12* Sharing Your Bread

REUEL JR. WAS AWAY FROM HOME on Thanksgiving Day for the first time. He was a freshman in college and couldn't make it home. In a letter to his parents, he wrote:

> We had a great day. The place really cleared out—only eight fellows left on our floor. We stayed up all night Wednesday night. Then we watched nine hours of football on TV. After that, we had a candlelight dinner. The fellows had to dress up. We really tried to make it nice— punch, nuts, mints, pecan rolls, and all the rest (frozen turkey dinners). So we survived. I hope to see you on December 7th. Will I be ready to come home!

Why did these eight fellows need to throw a party? The food was certainly not as good as their mothers prepared for their families. The table was not decorated with the same flair as the table back home. The dishes and silverware were the kind you would find in a dormitory. But they had to celebrate. Why?

Because of a tradition? Partly, of course. After all, it was Thanksgiving. The fellows had grown up in homes where the holiday was observed in certain traditional ways— roast turkey, cranberries, sweet potatoes, several kinds of vegetables, pumpkin pie, and so on. Behind the trimmings, there remained the event of a harvest Thanksgiving by the Pilgrims in 1621. So there was a tradition behind their party.

But wasn't there something more than tradition? In the new experience of being away from home, don't you think there was the need to find some appropriate way of explaining themselves to one another, of showing each other who they were? Even though they were away from home, they still belonged to particular families for whom this day was special. They had to celebrate.

The Need to Celebrate

Do you feel this need to celebrate? Whether you realize it or not, you are doing it all the time—if you are truly alive. You create your own small ceremonies by

laughing	kissing
crying	hitting
shouting	imitating

All of these are ways of expressing your own uniqueness, the importance of who you are and what you feel.

You also find ways of expressing who you are with others, as a member of groups to which you belong, whether family, school, church, or nation. But now your celebration becomes more involved. Someone has to organize it. Someone has to get the punch, nuts, mints, and pecan rolls. Someone has to set the table and light the candles, or whatever else you need to do to celebrate. But it is still the same, basic need to explain yourself to others in tangible, concrete ways.

The Joys of the Early Church

Look again at the first days of the church. Do you recall in the story of Pentecost some of the bystanders saying of the Christians: "They are filled with new wine"? That's a good description of the kind of spirit that must have been present. It was probably more like the victory celebration of a football team than most of the worship services we attend. They were celebrating because of Jesus—what God had done in him, was doing, and would do in the middle of their world. That was what brought them together as a People of God.

But they couldn't live in that high pitch of excitement forever. If what had happened to them was to continue, they had to find new ways of celebrating. The Acts of the Apostles says:

> "And they devoted themselves . . . to the breaking of bread and the prayers" (Acts 2:42).
> "And day by day, attending the temple together and breaking bread in their homes, they partook of food with glad and generous hearts" (Acts 2:46).

They continued to attend the Jewish temple and to offer their prayers in the way they were accustomed to doing. But that didn't seem adequate to express the new life they had come to know through Jesus. So they gathered in the homes of fellow believers for "the breaking of the bread." What did this mean?

Breaking Bread

(1) The simplest answer, of course, is that they needed to eat to live. They couldn't survive on inspiring experiences. They had to have bread for their stomachs. Eating their meals together was a means of providing food for those in the fellowship who were poor and didn't have enough to eat. On one occasion, Paul scolded the young church at Corinth because those who got there first ate everything up before the latecomers, who were poor slaves, arrived. He wanted everyone's hunger to be satisfied.

(2) Breaking bread was also the sign of Christian fellowship (koinonia, again). In fact, eating together at the same table signified brotherhood. Having once shared a meal, men could no longer be enemies. It was a tangible proof of friendship. For a Jew to eat at the same table with a Gentile was unheard of, but through Christ it was possible. Breaking bread together became a living demonstration of reconciliation.

(3) Breaking bread also provided a way of remembering Jesus, with whom they had eaten frequently when he was on earth. They remembered how he had broken bread and fed the hungry multitudes. They remembered in particular the meal on the night he was betrayed. He had taken bread, broken it, and given to them, commanding them to do this in remembrance of him and in anticipation of his coming kingdom. They also remembered the times after his resurrection when they had eaten with him and he had made himself known in the breaking of the bread. They needed to hear the story of Jesus, but they also needed to touch and taste it. The breaking of the bread brought back memories of how they had observed the

Lord's Supper. Before bread could be shared, it had to be broken. The act of breaking, therefore, reminded them of that event in which Jesus' body had been broken in sacrifice for them.

(4) Above all, the breaking of the bread became the occasion of celebrating and responding to the risen Jesus who was present in their midst. He was the one calling them together. He was also the one sending them out into the world to be his witnesses. This was why "they partook of food with glad and generous hearts." As his followers, they were being fed by him. When the bread was broken, he was with them again, present though unseen. They had to celebrate. In him the meaning of life broke through. Things seemed to come together. They knew who they were and what they were called to do. The Lord's Supper became for them a resurrection meal.

Public Service

The term which the early Christians borrowed from the Greek language to describe their worship is *leitourgia* (pronounced lay-tur-gee-ah). It can be translated "liturgy," which refers to a certain form of worship—the mass in a Roman Catholic church or the service in a Lutheran or Episcopal church, for example. But that doesn't quite fit the meaning of what the early Christians meant by the "breaking of the bread and the prayers." It seems to suggest something that takes place only at certain times, in particular places, and in prescribed ways.

Look for a moment at how the word *leitourgia* developed: (1) Originally, it meant the service which one freely rendered to the state or to the ruler. It might have been a public task such as building a road, serving in the army, performing in a dramatic play or athletic contest, or attending the ruler in his court. (2) Later on, it indicated the service which was required by law, such as compulsory military service. (3) Still later, it came to mean any work that a man might do as service to another man.

It would be more accurate to translate *leitourgia* as "the

people's work" or "public service," which suggests that worship, or the breaking of the bread, is not something restricted to the church building or services of worship. Rather, it includes the whole response of the People of God in work and worship to what God has done and is doing in Jesus.

An Illustration

Perhaps an illustration will help make the broader meaning of the word clear. When the early Christians gathered in homes for the breaking of the bread, they brought more food than was needed. After they had eaten their meal together and celebrated the Lord's Supper, they took the extra food and distributed it to the poor and needy in their fellowship. Their celebration would not have been complete apart from this act of public service, their *leitourgia*. In the act of distribution the Christ whom they had met in the breaking of bread could become real and tangible to others. This act was also their worship, their "liturgy."

Worship in Your Congregation

Now let's take a look at the worship in your congregation. What is there about your service on Sunday morning that suggests a celebration? How does your church perform its *leitourgia* during the week?

It might be helpful to summarize our response to God's deeds in Christ like this:

(1) To break bread together suggests that the People of God have a Sunday task. If worship is "the people's work," then it can't be left to the pastor and a few people in the choir while the rest sit back and watch. If worship is a real celebration of what God has done and is doing in Jesus, then everyone has to take part. You'll never find out who you are, where you belong, or what you are called to do as long as worship remains only a spectator sport. You have to get involved.

Whatever else you can do, you can always sing, pray, read, confess, and listen. This becomes your way of acting out who you are, of understanding yourself in relation to what God is doing. In so doing, you enter again into the night when he was betrayed, the darkness when he was crucified, the new dawn when he rose again from the dead. You sing your "Alleluia" because this is God's world and he will be victorious.

Worship begins as a Sunday affair, but it never stops there, not if it is the real thing. It must continue in the world outside.

(2) To break bread together suggests that the People of God have a daily task. They are called to go out into the world to distribute to someone else what they have received. They are being sent by Christ as carriers of his risen life to their neighbors. Having been fed, they are called to feed others. But let's be more specific:

> Your job as a student is also your liturgy. Your daily chores as a member of your family—washing windows, shoveling snow, cutting the grass, running errands—is also your liturgy. Your concern for a sick neighbor, your compassion for a mistreated minority, or the literal sharing of your bread with the hungry is also your liturgy.

In fact, there has been no real celebration without this public service.

Have you ever attended a Quaker service? You know that such a service can be a rather silent affair as the group waits upon the Spirit to enlighten someone and move him to speak. A Quaker once invited a Lutheran friend to a service. After the group had sat quietly for nearly thirty minutes, the Lutheran, who was accustomed to a planned service, became uneasy. He turned and whispered to his friend: "When does the service begin?" His Quaker friend, taken by surprise, responded: "Why, when the worship is over!"

Where is the real church found? Let's add to our previous clues these additional ones. The church is found

—wherever people gather around Jesus to celebrate the new life they have received in him

—wherever the bread is broken and distributed to the poor and needy

—wherever one's daily work is offered in service to God and one's neighbor.

Prayer

O Lord and heavenly Father, who gave to us your people the true Bread that comes down from heaven, even your Son Jesus Christ; grant that our souls may so be fed by him who gives life to the world, that we may abide in him and he in us, and your church be filled with the power of his unending life; through Jesus Christ our Lord. Amen.
—A New Prayer Book

Some Things To Do

1. Make a collage, drawing, folk song, poem, or prayer to express what it means to you to celebrate.

2. Illustrate through pictures from *Life, Look, Sports Illustrated*, photography, drawing, or some other media what you think the apostle Paul meant in 1 Corinthians 10:16: "Because there is one loaf, we who are many are one body, for we all partake of the same loaf."

3. Discuss in what ways the Sunday morning service is a celebration. How are the people actually involved? Does everyone get into the action? If people are only spectators, what can be done to improve the situation?

4. With resources your pastor can provide, give a report on the church year and its great festivals such as Christmas, Easter, and Pentecost, showing how these festivals and seasons provide occasions for celebration.

5. Study the hymn "O Brother Man, Fold to Thy Heart Thy Brother" and write an essay on how you can continue your worship in everyday affairs.

6. Be prepared to discuss in class these two illustrations:

a. Early in the civil rights struggle, the issue of concern was the desegregation of eating places. During a "sit-in" demonstration in Nashville in 1960, the home of the city's leading Negro lawyer was bombed. As a result 2000 students, Negro and white, marched in silent protest to the city hall. The mayor met them and ordered them to be cautious. Then, observing that their leader was a young minister, he appealed to the fact that they were Christians. "Let us pray together," he said. Then a voice from the crowd called out: "If you can pray together, why not eat together?"

Though he may not have been thinking of the Lord's Supper, discuss how it serves as a sign of reconciliation and peace. Was the voice from the crowd right?

b. In England there is a group of Christians associated with what is called "the house church movement." It came into being out of the recognition that there was a tragic separation of people's worship life from their daily life. Taking the second chapter of Acts, these Christians developed this program. One of the ministers of the church goes into the home of a workingman at 6:30 in the morning. Family and friends gather around the kitchen table. The minister reads the Bible, celebrates communion, using the bread that will later be eaten at breakfast.

Discuss whether or not you think this is a meaningful way of bringing worship and work closer together.

MEMORY WORK

What is the source of the church's life?

The life of the church has its source in God. It is created and renewed by his Spirit and Word, the holy sacraments, and prayer.

"There is one body and one Spirit, just as you were called to the one hope that belongs to your call, one Lord, one faith, one baptism, one God and Father of us all, who is above all and through all and in all" (*Ephesians 4:4–6*).

8

People for Others

The Servant of the Lord

Sunday	*Isaiah 42:1–9* Empowered to Serve
Monday	*Mark 10:35–45* Slave of All
Tuesday	*John 13:1–16* Pattern for All
Wednesday	*Philippians 2:5–11* The Mind of Christ
Thursday	*1 Corinthians 12:4–13* Different Gifts
Friday	*1 Corinthians 9:19–23* For the Sake of the Gospel
Saturday	*2 Corinthians 4:7–12* Weakness and Power

THE PASTOR wrote a list of trades and professions on the blackboard at the beginning of the confirmation class. Included on the list were the following:

chemist	doctor
banker	plumber
carpenter	waiter (waitress)
mechanic	nurse
garbage collector	politician
teacher	astronaut

He asked the members of the class to indicate two things:

(1) In your opinion, which is the most highly respected job? Tell why.
(2) Which is the least respected job? Tell why.

Before you read any farther, check what you think, using plus for the most respected and zero for the least respected. Be prepared to defend your answer.

In this group of students, the astronaut won over all the others as having the most highly respected job. The garbage collector and waiter (waitress) tied for last place. Why do you think they classified these persons like this? Your class might wish to discuss the response of these students as compared with your own.

It is interesting that when the class began to test their answers, especially with regard to the least respected jobs, they came up with these comments:

—unskilled workers are not as commanding of respect as highly skilled ones
—job opportunities for unskilled workers are limited
—unskilled jobs require hard work
—what would the community do without these services?

What do you think about their comments?

The mood of the discussion began to change when the pastor told the class that during his seminary career he had held two jobs: one as a waiter in a short-order restaurant and one as a night-watchman, which required hauling garbage from several floors of the building down to the alley, where it would be collected. By this time, one of the students rallied to the cause by suggesting that in New York City garbage collectors are called "sanitation engineers," wear neat uniforms, and drive white trucks with bucket seats.

The Form of a Servant

The reason for the sampling of opinion was to help the class to begin thinking about different forms of service people can render and to help them feel something of the scandal of what the New Testament means by "servant." The Greeks considered the work of a servant to be a very inferior sort of business. In one of Plato's dialogues, this question is raised: "How can a man be happy when he has to serve someone?" The Jews saw nothing unworthy in being a servant, especially if one was in the service of a greater master. But a lot of distinctions were made regarding who was worthy of being served and the rewards which one might expect as compensation for service rendered. You can imagine the surprise of the disciples on hearing Jesus say:

> . . . Whoever would be great among you must be your servant, and whoever would be first among you must be slave of all. For the Son of Man also came not to be served but to serve, and to give his life as a ransom for many   (Mark 10:43–45).

> Which is greater, one who sits at table or one who serves? Is it not the one who sits at table? But I am among you as one who serves   (Luke 22:27).

> If I then, your Lord and Teacher, have washed your feet, you also ought to wash one another's feet. For I have given you an example, that you also should do as I have done to you   (John 13:14, 15).

That was something new. And the reward was humiliation, suffering, and death.

A Servant People

Though we have gone a long way in glamorizing service in our society as something we admire, pay for, or reward, still Christians often stumble over

—being served by others, especially by their Lord
—placing themselves at the disposal of others without any thought of payment or reward

Indeed, this is the pattern of life for all who follow the Servant-Lord. Having received help through the love God has shown us in Christ, we want to help and serve others in something approaching the way in which we have been helped.

It is not surprising to read that the first Christians were characterized by their eagerness to render loving assistance to their neighbors. The worship (*leitourgia*) that began in the breaking of bread was continued in the distribution of food to those in need. It was the practical expression of Christian fellowship (*koinonia*) in which they had all things in common (Acts 2:44, 4:32). It was also the acting out of the Good News (*kerygma*).

But the young church hit a snag. In Acts 6:1–6, Luke reports that certain Greek widows were being neglected in the distribution of food by the church for the support of the poor in their own ranks. To correct the problem, it was decided that seven men be appointed to supervise the welfare program in order to leave the apostles free for preaching and teaching the Word. The name given to these men is "deacons," which comes from another Greek word, *diakonia* (pronounced dee-ak-oh-nee-ah). Its root meaning suggests waiting on tables. In a broader sense, it refers to the act of bearing burdens for somebody else as a direct result of the loving service of Jesus Christ. It can even include the offering of one's life for others.

You might say it was unfortunate that the twelve apostles had to cut themselves off from this kind of table service and had to "specialize." Stephen, we recall, was able both to feed people and to preach the Good News.

Do you ever think of the church's ministry as waiting on tables? What would this mean in terms of the relationship of the church to the world? Someone has suggested that Christ invites all men, including the church, to his banquet table. The only distinction between the guests is that while the world is called to partake of God's feast without obligation, the church is called to serve tables and wash the dishes after all have been fed. Do you like this way of thinking about the church as a servant People?

Another Illustration

Paul, you recall, was so excited about what he had to tell people that he traveled everywhere he could. If he had owned a Jeep, he would have had a broken axle half the time. One of the things he was telling the people about was the church. This was all new to them, especially to the Greeks, and so he had to explain it.

He said the church was like their bodies. Even the poorest of them had a body. As these people looked down at their dusty big toes sticking out of their sandals, he explained that just as each part of the body has a job to do, so does each member of the church. As they flexed their brown arms, he told them:

> Now you are the body of Christ and individually members of it   (1 Corinthians 12:27).

That is to say, you are one of Christ's hands or feet to do his work in the world. You are bound to every other member just as your hands and feet are bound to the rest of your body. All members of the body of Christ are bound to one another and to the head of the body, Jesus Christ. How do you like this way of thinking about the church as a servant People?

What Body Means

The average church member would probably be shocked if he thought through the implications of this way of understanding who he is and what he is called to do. Perhaps it might help you to think about what this means in terms of your service both in the church and in the world. Here are some suggestions:

(1) To be a body is to be physical. You never need to apologize or feel ashamed of that. You live in a body, or you wouldn't be alive. Remember this when you think about the church as the body of Christ. It's more, of course, than you and your body. But it is you together with other bodies. God's mission in the world wouldn't get very far if it depended on men's spirits.

What would your Sunday morning worship be like if people were there only in spirit, while their bodies were lounging in bed, or lying on the beach, or chasing after a golf ball? You can worship God wherever you are, of course. But if you are going to celebrate God's gracious deeds in Christ as something you do together, you have to occupy space on a wooden bench where you open your mouth, sing, pray, and confess.

So with our service in the world. The church has to be a physical body and not just a beautiful idea. It has to occupy space on earth. It has to be found where people are. It has to care about the needs of people in order to be faithful to its mission. The body of Christ is a physical body.

(2) The church as the body of Christ must be a living body that moves and acts. You can't get the dishes done or the lawn cut by thinking positive thoughts or by having good intentions. You have to roll up your sleeves and get your body moving. So with the body of Christ. You recognize it by what it does, not for itself but for others. Its resolutions and official statements at annual meetings or church conferences mean nothing unless something comes of it in concrete, tangible deeds.

But what does the body of Christ do? How does it serve?

When Jesus began his ministry, he took for his marching orders the words of Isaiah:

> The Spirit of the Lord is upon me, because he has anointed me to preach good news to the poor. He has sent me to proclaim release to the captives and recovering of sight to the blind, to set at liberty those who are oppressed, to proclaim the acceptable year of the Lord (Luke 4:18, 19).

These are also the things which the exalted Jesus of Nazareth continues to do through us as members of his body if we are faithful to him who is the head of the body.

(3) The members of the body do not all have the same function. Read again how Paul describes the different parts of the body (1 Corinthians 12:14–31). How many different kinds of members does he mention? How many different kinds of work does he say need to be done by these members? Notice that he doesn't leave any loopholes for anyone—as if a member of the body might goof off, do nothing, or simply exist as decoration.

Everyone has something he can do. Not all can teach or preach. (Aren't you glad for that?) Paul says: "If all were a single organ, where would the body be?" (verse 19). But all can help in some way to serve the needs of men. Some serve in business. Some by farming. Some serve in labor unions. Some in home-making. Some serve by being "sanitation engineers." Some by being astronauts.

How do you serve? You are a student. School is where you spend the most of your time. It is the place where important attitudes and concepts are being formed. It is also where most of your friends are. What does it mean to be the body of Christ where you are now? You will have to answer that. But it will most likely be determined by the needs you see and by your ability to respond to those needs.

There is something only you can do. You live where adults cannot really enter except as strangers. You have a unique relationship with other young people. You also have the opportunity to speak out on issues that are relevant to your school. The point is simply this:

You are important.
You have a unique gift.
You are called to serve where you are.

But whether a hand or a foot, a mouth or a big toe, each one is called to do his work in the world. It is the service that matters!

(4) The members of the body must be co-ordinated. Can you imagine an argument like this going on in your eye?

Cornea: You would never see a thing except for the fact that I am so clear.

Iris: No, you're all wrong. I am superior because I adjust the pupil so that it is just right.

Lens: Now wait a minute! If it weren't for me, the light wouldn't be collected at all. You would all be in the dark.

Retina: But I have the last word. You would never see "her" or "him" or "it" if I didn't form the image right here!

Wouldn't that be a senseless argument? Yet you often find this kind of competition within the body of Christ, making the church a poor servant in the world. The world looks at Christians, fighting and bickering among themselves, and says: "Why can't you guys get organized?"

The places where the church must serve are many and are constantly changing. No one part of the church can possibly do the whole job all by itself. What is required is a co-ordination of efforts so that we are not trying to go in all directions at once and never getting anywhere as a consequence. This co-ordination will mean at least two things:

(1) a dynamic give-and-take with all other Christians for the sake of the mission of serving the world

(2) a closer working relationship with non-Christians who are deeply involved in the struggle for freedom and justice for the good of all men

When this happens, the church as the body of Christ can become what it is called to be, the servant of God and men.

Summing Up

Now let's take a long look over our shoulder to see where we have been, what we have discovered about the church, and what it means to belong to the church. I hope that you now are beginning to see the church as something more than a building, an organization, people who are alike, a refuge from the world, your pastor, a monument to the past, and so on. Rather, I hope you can see it, rejoice in it, participate in it

(1) wherever the Good News concerning Jesus is being proclaimed and lived out
(2) wherever people are being drawn together in one body, by one Spirit
(3) wherever people gathered around Jesus are celebrating, breaking the bread and distributing it to others
(4) wherever men take upon themselves the problems and needs of others, living, struggling, hoping together.

Look again at the first page of your notebook, the "Who Am I?" page. Is there anything you would like to add? Would your belonging to the People of God make any significant changes in what you think, feel, hope, or do? Would it in any way help the real "you" to come through loud and clear?

Prayer

I am no longer my own, but yours. Put me to what you will, rank me with whom you will; put me to doing, put me to suffering; let me be employed for you or laid aside for you, exalted for you or brought low for you; let me be full, let me be empty; let me have all things, let me have nothing; I freely and heartily yield all things to your pleasure and disposal.

And now, O glorious and blessed God, Father, Son, and Holy Spirit, you are mine, and I am yours. So be it. And the covenant which I have made on earth, let it be ratified in heaven. Amen.

—John Wesley

O Lord Jesus! forasmuch as your Way is narrow and is also much despised in the world, give me grace to bear gladly the despisings of the world. There is no servant greater than his Lord, nor any disciple above his Master. Let your servant therefore be exercised in your ways, for therein is health and the very perfection of life; whatsoever I read or hear beside that Way, it refreshes me not, nor delights me fully.

—Thomas á Kempis

Some Things To Do

1. Write a paper about one of the following great Christians whose lives exemplify service to men:

   Francis of Assisi   Paul Carlson
   Dag Hammarsköld   William Stringfellow
   Albert Schweitzer   Toyohiko Kagawa
   Martin Luther King   Frank Laubach

2. A famous theologian has said that the mission of the church is to participate in God's action, which is "to make and to keep life human." What do you think about this? Do you agree? Complete the following, using one sentence for each statement:

   My definition of the church is . . .

   As I see it, the church's primary mission is . . .

3. Discuss (a) whether or not most churches are more concerned with maintaining their own programs than serving the needs of the community; (b) whether the churches in your community seem to be interested in competing with each other or co-operating.

4. Do some research on your congregation's purpose and mission. (Your pastor can make available such things as the church's constitution, annual report, budget, etc.)

   a. List the church officers and the duties of each.

   b. Make an appointment to interview one of the officers of the church or members of the board to discuss the following questions:

   1. What are the working goals of the congregation?

   2. What are the problems the congregation faces?

   c. Study the church budget in the light of its mission as the body of Christ:

   1. How much is spent yearly on maintaining the building and church properties: salaries of the church staff—pastor, organist, choir director, custodian, secretary, etc.? How much for music and other things to help in the worship service? How much for the church's program of educating children and adults?

   2. How much is spent for the mission outside the local congregation? for missions? for world relief?

   d. Discuss with your pastor how he understands his task and how he spends his time.

   e. Are there particular aspects of work that are being neglected by your congregation? What are these? What can young people do about them?

   f. Find out how decisions are made in your congregation. Are there any opportunities for young people to engage in acts of decision-making in your congregation?

5. Select one of the following statements you would like the class to discuss:

a. "Rarely do our words arouse amazement, but people look up when they meet a free person who uses that freedom to serve." [1]

b. "Really to help another person is one of the hardest things one can do. It takes thought. It takes self-discipline. It takes courage and humility. But all too often in the church it has been assumed that all it takes is good intentions. To be honest, a great deal of so-called Christian helping is one of three things. It is either impulsive, or moralistic, or it is undertaken not really to help another but to satisfy the conscience, the need to control or to be thanked of the person giving help." [2]

c. "More important, we need a new definition of the pastoral role of the clergyman. In effect, as pastor the minister is called to give time to prepare and equip the members for their ministries in the church and in the world." [3]

d. "If the training of a football team were limited to chalk talks in the classroom, the team would be quite ineffective when the time came to play the game. In fact, there might not be any players left, since it would be difficult to keep the interest of a team if they were never taken out on the field. The church's training of the laity seldom gets beyond the classroom. No matter how clever or interesting our chalk talks, there is no substitute for actual experience in the field." [4]

[1] J. C. Hoekendijk, *The Church Inside Out,* (Westminster Press, 1964), p. 88.
[2] Alan Keith Lucas, *This Difficult Business of Helping,* (C.L.C., 1965), p. 4.
[3] George W. Webber, *The Congregation in Mission,* (Abingdon Press, 1964), pp. 65–66.
[4] Loren E. Halvorson, *Exodus into the World,* (Augsburg Publishing House, 1966), p. 65.

MEMORY WORK

First Article of the Apostles' Creed

I believe in God the Father almighty, Maker of heaven and earth.

What does this mean?

I believe that God has created me and all that exists. He has given me and still preserves my body and soul with all their powers.

He provides me with food and clothing, home and family, daily work, and all I need from day to day. God also protects me in time of danger and guards me from every evil.

All this he does out of fatherly and divine goodness and mercy, though I do not deserve it.

Therefore I surely ought to thank and praise, serve and obey him.

This is most certainly true.

O Jesus, I Have Promised

O Jesus, I have promised To serve Thee to the end;
Be Thou forever near me, My Master and my Friend:
I shall not fear the battle If Thou art by my side,
Nor wander from the pathway If Thou wilt be my Guide.

O let me feel Thee near me! The world is ever near;
I see the sights that dazzle, The tempting sounds I hear;
My foes are ever near me, Around me and within;
But, Jesus, draw Thou nearer, And shield my soul from sin.

O let me hear Thee speaking In accents clear and still,
Above the storms of passion, The murmurs of self-will!
O speak to reassure me, To hasten or control!
O speak, and make me listen, Thou Guardian of my soul!

O Jesus, Thou hast promised To all who follow Thee
That where Thou art in glory There shall Thy servant be;
And, Jesus, I have promised To serve Thee to the end;
O give me grace to follow, My Master and my Friend!
  Amen.

—The Hymnal

Unit 3

Do You Promise?

Photo by Varde

9

Promises
to Keep

Promises to Keep

Sunday	*Psalm 116* True Gratitude
Monday	*Ecclesiastes 5:1–7* Honest Words
Tuesday	*Matthew 5:33–37* Yes and No
Wednesday	*Deuteronomy 6:4–9* The Great Commandment
Thursday	*Romans 13:1–10* Love Your Neighbor
Friday	*Matthew 7:24–27* Hearers and Doers
Saturday	*Philippians 3:7–16* One Thing I Do

CAN YOU RECALL any occasions when you have either spoken or heard any of the following words used by others?

> "Cross my heart and hope to die"
> "I give you my word."
> "Trusting in the grace of God for this task, do you promise to accept these responsibilities?"
> "With God's help, I will."
> "And I do promise and covenant before God and these witnesses . . ."
> "Do you promise to make diligent use of the means of grace to continue in the peace and fellowship of the people of God, and with the aid of the Holy Spirit to be Christ's faithful disciple to your life's end?"

You probably used the first statement as a child. You may use the second statement on frequent occasions now. The other statements are more ceremonial. You have undoubtedly heard them in church. Some of these statements you will use yourself someday. Can you guess the solemn moments these vows or words of promise celebrate? They are taken from *A Book of Worship for Covenant Churches* in this sequence:

> Statement three from "An Order for Infant Baptism" (p. 58)
> Statement four from "The Service of Confirmation" (p. 156)
> Statement five from "The First Order of Marriage" (p. 88)
> Statement six from "An Order for Adult Baptism" (p. 64)

Man As a Promise-Maker

What makes statements like these necessary? A part of the mystery of being you is that you are a promise-maker. It is one requirement which is written into the very fabric of your life. Apart from this requirement we could not live as responsible persons within all the complex relationships of society. Even the switchblade gang has its vows, which, incidentally, are often taken more seriously and require more discipline than the vows of religious organizations. But whether good or bad, man as he is created in the image of God is a promise-maker.

Life Needs to Be Organized

Making promises is a way of getting life organized. A person makes a vow because he feels he must bring the several interests and concerns of his life together around some central core of meaning or loyalty. It belongs to good housekeeping. The memory of a vow once taken calls a person to stand at attention. It reminds him of his primary loyalty.

All of us are constantly doing battle with those unruly elements in ourselves which tempt us to take the path of least resistance. For this reason we need to bind ourselves to causes greater than ourselves, to loyalties that command us, that make us one with ourselves. To be a real person—in contrast to being only an animal living by sheer instinct—is to have the ability to make and keep promises, to choose some cause that has chosen you, to live in a relationship of promises and covenants.

Conserving the Best

Making promises is also a way of conserving the best in life. By making a vow a person puts the reins of his will onto the best of his feelings so that something good may come of it. Here, for example, is the gift of life bestowed on two parents in their newborn child, a mystery so great that they simply stand in wonder before it and say, "Thank you, God." But that is not enough. They see in their child the high calling to become what he was created to be, a child of God. So they bundle him up and take him into the house of God to pay their vows. That is, they make promises as parents that they will do everything in their power to see that he becomes what he has been created to be. In so doing, they receive the assurance that comes from knowing they are not alone in this task, that the congregation, as well as the Lord himself, will be assisting them. Just so this rich moment of celebration can be remembered.

Throughout life, our finest moments are celebrated in the giving and receiving of promises—

baptism
confirmation
church membership
marriage—

as well as the yearly festivals and seasons of the Christian year such as Advent, Christmas, Lent, Easter, and Pentecost that help us to remember the mighty acts of God.

We Live With Others

Promises are also made in recognition that one does not live apart from others but with others. One makes a vow, not only to God but to men as well.

In the sacrament of baptism, the congregation listens to the vows and takes vows as the pastor asks: "Do you promise with God's help . . . ?" In the service of confirmation, the pastor asks each confirmand in the presence of the congregation: "Do you promise . . . ?" In the reception of new members into the church, the congregation is present as the pastor asks: "Do you promise to join us in worship and service . . . ?"

In the wedding service, the friends of the bride and groom are there, not as spectators, but as witnesses to the solemn vows: "I do promise before God and these witnesses. . . ." Promises are solemn and binding because we live continually before and with others who will remember and see if we are as good as our word.

Something God Requires

Finally, making promises is something God requires. The First Commandment begins: "I am the Lord thy God. . . ." There is not another person in the whole world who can require the kind of total obedience God requires. In fact, nothing can inspire loyalty and dependability as do power and faithfulness. When a person forgets God in the making of a promise, he has lost the strength of the promise. The presence and authority of God are the ultimate power in any promise.

To What Shall I Be Loyal?

But now let's talk about you. You are involved right now in seeking to discover who you are and what you want as a full human being. Whether or not it is clear who you are, you know you are somebody. But there are other questions crowding in on you too:

> If I can find out who I am, then to what do I plan to give myself? To what or whom shall I be loyal? What is worth serving that will not betray me?

Here is a working hypothesis or proposition for you to consider:

> What you choose to be loyal to and belong to shapes the fate of the one life which is yours.

Do you agree? Would you like to test it out? Try it on for size. It is in your power to decide for what causes, for what purposes, for whose sake you will invest your life. Your confirmation course offers you this live option within which to anchor your life:

> First, you can know yourself at your best as a Christian and member of the People of God.
> Second, the service of the People of God in the world

is something you can give yourself to without any reservations in the certainty that in this kind of activity the meaning and depth of life can be found.

Joining the People of God

For the past few months you have been studying the story of the People of God, and now, more recently, the church and what it is meant to be and do. Hopefully, you are now ready to ask: How do I become a member?

In one sense, you are already a part of the People of God. When you were born, you didn't apply for membership in your family. You were simply welcomed into the family by reason of your birth. So with the church. Most of you have been loved by your church from the time you were born. Even if your parents have not been close to the church, you are nevertheless special to it. As one teacher of a Sunday-school class for Junior-Highs put it:

> There has always been a place here in the church where you were wanted and welcome. Now we continue to try to show our love and concern by our teaching you, but also by our support of your projects—your bake sales, car washes, etc. We are happy when you succeed, and our hearts hurt with yours when you fail or have a sorrow.

So, you see, you already belong in a very important way. But because we believe your decision to belong to the People of God should be your own, there are normally two steps which the Covenant Church considers important:

Step One: Confirmation

The word "confirm" means to strengthen or make firm. It is tied up with the promises made at your baptism.

If you were baptized as an infant, you are encouraged as a result of your study to confess publicly on the day of confirmation your faith in Jesus Christ, thereby saying "Yes" to your part of God's promises made to you. These promised are strengthened or made firm by your decision.

If you have not been baptized, you are also encouraged to confess your faith in Jesus Christ, to receive Christian baptism, and thereby to become a disciple in whom God's promises are coming true.

In either case, the promises you make when you are confirmed are solemn and binding, acknowledging the fact that you do indeed confess faith in Jesus Christ and that you find in him the clue to who you are and in what direction you intend to go. Your pastor will say something like this:

> "As a consequence of this study, you have been confronted by Jesus Christ and challenged to accept him as your Savior and Lord. Throughout your lives you will be called upon to make many important decisions. The decision you are now given opportunity to affirm is one of the most sacred you will ever be called upon to declare. By it you confess your Christian faith and make significant and sacred promises to God and his church. I therefore ask you to affirm your faith in the words of the Apostles' Creed. Do you believe in God? . . . ." [1]

Right now some of these promises may seem like stepping into a suit of clothes two sizes too big. Or maybe even like a medieval suit of armor. But take heart. Some of us who long ago made similar promises are still growing up to them.

You should know, of course, that the church doesn't expect you to make promises you don't intend to keep. But if your heart is leaning in the right direction, that's what matters. And the church, like your best friend, will wait for you, pray for you, even shelter you until your head catches up with your heart. Whatever you promise, be faithful to your inner soul.

Step Two: Joining the Church

"But when I'm confirmed, don't I become a member of the church?" In many churches, you would become what is

---

[1] *A Book of Worship for Covenant Churches* (Chicago: Covenant Press, 1964), p. 155.

called "a full communicant member." In the Covenant Church, we give the members of the confirmation class time to catch their breath before taking the final vows of membership. We believe that this serves as a reminder that confirmation is not a graduation but only a beginning. You might think of it like this:

> Confirmation is like learning to drive. You take driving lessons, learn all about road signs, speed limits, plus good etiquette behind the wheel. The responsibility of driving is impressed on you. Then, because you have learned the ground rules and are eager to drive, you apply for your driver's liscense. Church membership is like driving the car on your own so that you can move about more freely—not simply where you want to go but where God sends you.

Or you might think of it like this: You say in confirmation who you are and to whom you belong. You say in church membership what you intend to do about it, what your part will be in serving the mission of the church. Both steps constitute your commissioning for responsible service. More than anything else the church wants to hear you say:

> "Here I am. My boot-camp training is over. I am ready to be scnt out on active duty."

What the Church Expects

The rest of this study looks ahead to what follows your confirmation vows and seeks to spell out more precisely what it is you promise. Here are the questions to which you will be asked to respond when you join the church:

> Do you believe the Bible to be the Word of God and the only perfect rule for faith, doctrine, and conduct?
>
> Do you confess Jesus Christ as your Savior and Lord?

Do you purpose to remain steadfast in the faith unto the end and as a true follower of Jesus Christ to walk in newness of life?

Do you promise in watchfulness and prayer to diligently use the Word of God and the Holy Sacraments?

Do you promise to join us in worship and service and to give regularly of your substance for the work of the gospel as carried on by this church and the denomination to which it belongs?

You can begin to see that the church has a firmness about it. Not just anything goes. It is a group that holds you responsible and makes some demands on you. If you are going to participate as a member of the People of God, something is required of you as a promise-maker. But you wouldn't want it any other way, would you?

Prayer

Give us
A pure heart
That we may see Thee,
A humble heart
That we may hear Thee,
A heart of love
That we may serve Thee,
A heart of faith
That we may live Thee,

Thou
Whom I do not know
But Whose I am.
Thou
Whom I do not comprehend
But Who hast dedicated me
To my fate.
Thou—
      —Dag Hammarsköld [2]

---

[2] Dag Hammarsköld, *Markings*, (New York: Alfred A. Knopf, 1964), p. 214.

Some Things To Do

1. Make a list of the things you desire and value most in life and tell what you plan to do with your life. Then make a list of the things you think the church expects of you and hopes you will do with your life. Are the lists similar in any way? Different? Discuss the point of tension and indicate how these two lists and the tensions relate to confirmation and church membership.

2. List the groups that are open to you. Indicate the requirements for belonging. Which do you accept and value most? Which accepts and values you most? Who determines who can join?

3. Study the following passage in depth: Mark 8:34–36. First, use whatever resources you can find to understand what it means. Then write out your own translation of the verses. Try not to use any of the phrases that appear in the Revised Standard Version but use your own words. Having completed that, answer the following questions: (a) If I took these verses seriously, what would it mean for me right now? (b) Would this involve doing anything differently? (c) What would I care about most?
   Be prepared to share your translation and thoughts about the passage (Mark 8:34–36) with the rest of the class.

4. Outline the procedures necessary for becoming a member of your congregation. Talk it over with your parents and interview the chairman of the board of deacons. You may wish to ask this question: What is expected of those who become members of your congregation? In the light of this assignment, answer the following questions: (a) Do the requirements for church membership correspond in any way to Mark 8:34–36? (b) Do you think the "price of admission" is too high or too low in your congregation? (c) Is there any cost to continue as a member? (d) How does a person lose his membership in the church?

5. Read the following quotations:

   (a) "I don't know Who—or what—put the question, I don't know when it was put. I don't even remember answering. But at some moment I did answer Yes to Someone—or Something—and from that hour I was certain that existence is meaningful and that, therefore, my life, in self-surrender, had a goal." [3]

—Dag Hammarskjöld on Pentecost Sunday, 1961

(b) "I looked up daily to the Son of God, who in the garden of Gethsemane had surrendered to the difficult and holy will of God, who through his agony and conflict had robbed death of its fears. From him I learned to endure trembling and anguish, and to say 'Yes' to this difficult holy will of God." [4]

—Hans Lilje, a German church leader who opposed the Nazis during World War II and was imprisoned

Be prepared to discuss these statements. What do you think they mean and how are they related to their experience?

[3] *Ibid.*, p. 205.
[4] Hans Lilje, *The Valley of the Shadow*, (Muhlenberg Press, 1950), p. 91.

MEMORY WORK

Who is God?

God is personal, eternal Spirit, Father of our Lord Jesus Christ, and our Father.

"For from him and through him and to him are all things. To him be glory for ever. Amen." (*Romans 11:36*).

What does it mean to be a man?

To be a man is to be created in the likeness of God, free and responsible in relation to God, the world, neighbor, and self.

"Thou hast made him little less than God, and dost crown him with glory and honor. Thou hast given him dominion over the works of thy hands; thou hast put all things under his feet" (*Psalm 8:5, 6*).

Photo by Varde

10

The Word from God

The Presence of the Word

Sunday	*Psalm 19* The Works and Word of God
Monday	*Nehemiah 8:1–8* Hearing the Word
Tuesday	*Luke 8:4–15* The Good Seed
Wednesday	*James 1:22–25* The Mirror of the Word
Thursday	*2 Timothy 3:10–17* Wise unto Salvation
Friday	*Romans 10:5–13* The Word is Near
Saturday	*1 Samuel 3:1–14* Thy Servant Hears

WHAT DO YOU THINK the world will be like in 2000 A.D?

Not long ago several distinguished scientists (not science-fiction writers or sensational journalists) addressed themselves to this question and came up with these visions of the future:

—trips to the moon will be commonplace
—man-made satellites will be inhabited
—all food will be synthetic
—world's population will be four times as large as now
—sea water and rocks will provide all necessary metals
—disease and famine will have been eliminated
—knowledge will be accumulated in "electronic books"
—knowledge will be transmitted directly to the nervous system by coded messages
—reading and learning mountains of information will no longer be necessary, and so on. . . .[1]

This will be your world. And it's beginning to take shape right now. A paradise? Life certainly sounds a lot easier. What part appeals to you the most? The part about books and learning? One communications expert, Marshall McLuhan, has pointed out that we have already moved beyond the printed page (books, magazines, newspapers) as the major tool of learning to sight and sound—radio, TV, movies, recordings, audio and video tape, and programmed instruction. This changes not only our habits but the way we think about life. There was a time not too long ago when people had to read books and newspapers to know what was going on in other parts of the world. They had time to evaluate what they read, to reflect on it, and to sort out the meanings of things. Now, however, we are almost immediately aware of what is happening all over the world. The sights and sounds of death and destruction, of quiet heroism and courageous deeds, are alive for even the youngest child. You get the feeling of being involved. You are there where the action is.

---

[1] Adapted from Jacques Ellul in *The Technological Society.*

Why the Bible?

Doesn't it seem rather odd and a bit old-fashioned that in this kind of changing world the first question the church asks of you when you become a member is:

> "Do you believe the Bible to be the Word of God, the only perfect rule for faith, doctrine, and conduct?"

Isn't the world of the Bible out of touch with the world that is coming to be? Perhaps it sounds to you like a telephone directory with hard-to-pronounce names connected by an endless string of "begats." Or maybe it sounds trite and overfamiliar because you have heard a lot of stories about bath-robed patriarchs, camel trains, and voices out of the blue that seem to have little direct bearing on you. Why then does the church still put a question like this at the top of the list?

What Makes the Bible Special

Do we keep the Bible around because people have nostalgia for a best-seller? Or because its somber cover and gold edges seem to set it apart from other books and add a touch of reverence to our homes? Or because it makes a nice present when we are confirmed?

There are many reasons why the Bible is so special. Perhaps we could summarize by saying that the Bible is special to the church and to Christians in general because it deals authentically with life, real life as we must live it. It speaks to real problems we all have, problems like fear, guilt, and death. It speaks in a plain, blunt, no-nonsense way that makes sense. It helps us get our bearings by showing us the goal or purpose of our life, always reminding us that God has a purpose and works with us to obtain it. And when we get off course, it tells us that this same God is always there to forgive us and put us back on the right track.

One theologian puts it like this:

"There are Bibles because there are Christians. There are Christians because of the Bible." [2]

What do you think he means? Do you agree? It goes almost without saying that without the story of the Bible—its shared memory of events and happenings both in Israel and in Jesus Christ—we would find it hard to know God and to understand what life is all about. That's why the Bible is the church's book and why the church speaks of the Bible as the Word of God. God has something to say to us!

Word As Event

But what does the church mean by the word of God? In order to understand what it means, we must try to think our way back to a time when there were fewer words than there are now. We recall that the Bible began among a people who had no written documents or books such as we have but only the memory of spoken words. When a man said, "I give you my word," it was taken just as seriously as a modern legal contract drawn up by a lawyer. Words were sacred.

Among such a people, God's word carried an even more powerful meaning. When the Hebrews spoke of the world's coming into being, they did so in terms of God's speaking his word.

"God said, 'Let there be light;' and there was light"
(Genesis 1:3)
"Let all the world fear the Lord, let all the inhabitants of the world stand in awe of him! For he spoke, and it came to be; he commanded, and it stood forth"
(Psalm 33:8, 9).
"For as the rain and the snow come down from heaven, and return not thither but water the earth, making it bring forth and sprout, giving seed to the sower and

---

[2] Emil Brunner, *Our Faith* (New York: Scribners, 1954), p. 7.

bread to the eater, so shall my word be that goes forth
from my mouth; it shall not return to me empty"

(Isaiah 55:10, 11)

There is, in fact, no difference between a word spoken and
a deed done. God's word is the way he gets things done. It's
not just talk but action. He speaks in the language of
events—

creation
an exodus
an exile
a conquest
a defeat

Word As Message

The word of God has another meaning closely related to
the first. The Old Testament prophets were men who spoke
for God. Over and over again you hear in their proclamation one word coming through loud and clear: "Thus says
the Lord." That doesn't mean that the prophets heard God
speak to them in sentences so that if you had been there
with a tape recorder you could have caught the sound of
someone speaking. Rather, it means that the prophets had
the right word for the situation—that single thrust of
truth, whether of hurt or healing, that went straight to the
heart of the matter. They told it like it was so that the
meaning of what God was doing could become clear for all
to see and understand.

Listen to how the prophet Jeremiah describes his encounter with the word:

"Now the word of the Lord came to me saying, 'Before I
formed you in the womb I knew you, and before you
were born I consecrated you; I appointed you a prophet
in the nations.' Then I said, 'Ah, Lord God! Behold,
I do not know how to speak, for I am only a youth.'
But the Lord said to me, 'Do not say, "I am only a youth";
for to all to whom I send you you shall go, and whatever

I command you you shall speak. . . . Behold, I have put
my words in your mouth. See, I have set you this day over
nations and over kingdoms, to pluck up and to break
down, to destroy and to overthrow, to build and to plant' "
(Jeremiah 1:5–7, 9–10).

Because God's power was present in his message, something happened. When he proclaimed God's judgment on
the Israelites for breaking their part in the covenant, two
things occurred:

First, his message forced men to take sides. The
priests became very angry and condemned him as a
traitor. Others, however, came to his defense, recog-
nizing in his message an authentic voice from the
Lord. (See Jeremiah 26:11 ff.)

Second, the judgment he announced happened. The
word finally came true because God was present in the
message he proclaimed.

So in the New Testament. When the early Christians
told the Good News about Jesus, the Book of Acts refers to
their preaching and teaching—both what they said and
what they did—as "the word." Again, something happened. Luke says that Peter's message on the Day of Pentecost stung his hearers to the heart. Then followed repentance, baptism, and entrance into the Christian fellowship.
Those who joined the church were taught, they belonged to
each other, they broke bread together, they prayed, and
they served one another.

The word is not empty talk. It changes and creates the
People of God.

Word As Person

The word of God refers also to Jesus of Nazareth. When
other attempts at communicating with men had failed and
they had rejected the message of the prophets, God himself

came in Jesus. The first chapter of John tells us at least two things:

> First, through the word the world was created.

> "In the beginning was the Word, and the Word was with God, and the Word was God. He was in the beginning with God; all things were made through him, and without him was not anything made that was made" (John 1:1–3).

> Second, the word became a person.

> "And the Word became flesh and dwelt among us, full of grace and truth; we have beheld his glory, glory as of the only Son from the Father" (John 1:14).

In Jesus Christ God's word—his power, his intention—became personally present, made flesh in the deed of a single human life, living among men, dying and rising again and ever-living. We shall have more to say of him later.

Word As Written

The word of God as event, as message, and as person makes the Bible special, the most important book of the church. In the Bible we have the written record of how God's word has been heard and acted on by men of faith. Here we have a first-hand, on-the-spot, eye-witness account of how men have encountered and responded to God and what he has been doing in the world. This doesn't mean that when the Bible was gathered into a single book such as we have now and made the official book of the church that God suddenly stopped speaking and acting. It does mean, however, that without this first and primary record we would find it very difficult to decide which of the many words we hear today bring with them the word or power of God. We would also find it hard to understand what God's purpose for our world today is and what he is calling his people to be and do. We would also be without that final, saving word which he has spoken in Jesus Christ.

The Enduring Word

But will the Bible still be valid in 2000 A.D.? Yes, as long as people are asking such questions as these:

Who am I?

To what can I give myself that is dependable and trustworthy?

What is the meaning of life?

Who is God?

What is his purpose for us? for the world?

Can sin and death be overcome?

What must we do to be saved?

The word of God, whether written down in a book or transmitted directly to the nervous system by coded message, remains the word for all time. It was true back then, and it is true now. It answered questions back then, and it is answering them now. It brought comfort to slaves and exiles then and still does so. Someone has said that "the prophets and the Gospels (the Bible) are still before us and not behind us." The faith which the Bible expresses still stretches our hearts and minds. We still have a long way to go before we catch up to its truth.

This is why the church asks this question first: "Do you believe the Bible to be the Word of God . . . ?" In effect, it is asking: Are you ready to stretch your hearts and minds, to undertake the pilgrimage of faith and understanding, to have your life judged, corrected, and re-shaped by God's message? Are you willing to let this word help you to keep your eyes open to life as it is today? Are you prepared to do some hard thinking that will lead to courageous acting in serving God's purpose in the world?

Prayer

Grant, my Lord, that I be wise enough to seek on the journey of life the deep wisdom of the Holy Bible.

Make it a spur to my weakness, a trumpet call to my flagging will, a cleansing rebuke to my sins.

Let it lift my eyes from the dark borders of sin and pain to the upper levels of faith and consecration.

Let it reveal to me the glory of goodness and the beauty of the unselfish spirit.

Fuse its principles of living with my daily decisions.

Thread its spirit through my thoughts.

Calm and empower me by its poetry.

Through the rise and fall of nations, teach me its eternal truth that "righteousness exalteth a nation but sin is a reproach to any people."

Enlarge the purpose for which I live in its vision of a new and better age for this our world.

Through it reveal unto me the wisdom and power of One in whom we find thyself.

Grant me, O God, the guidance of the Bible. Amen.
—Percy R. Hayward [3]

Some Things To Do

1. Select favorite or interesting stories which have been told and retold in your family about things involving parents, or grandparents, or other relatives. Share them with the class. In relation to these stories, think about these questions: (a) What place do memories have in your life? (b) What things do you remember most vividly? (c) IIow do these mcmories influence your life? (d) Do the memories of your parents have any importance to you?

---

[3] Percy R. Hayward, *Young People's Prayers* (New York: Association Press, 1950), p. 50.

2. Learn to sing with the help of the class "A Ballad of Holy History." Answer the following questions:

   a. What is a ballad?

   b. How many incidents from the Scriptures are found in this ballad?

   c. Are there any other stories or events which might have been included?

   d. Which of the four songs of sin strike you as most relevant to the church today? to the nation?

   e. Why is the first verse repeated at the end of the ballad?

3. Listen to folk songs that express anger. (a) What is the singer angry about? (b) Does he offer any solutions? (c) Is he in any way like the Old Testament prophets? (d) Could he be speaking God's word? (e) Can you name any other people in our time who might be called prophets— people in government, news media, arts and sciences, as well as in the church?

4. Complete the following, using action words:

Home is _____	Happiness is _____
Love is _____	Hope is _____
Friendship is _____	Peace is _____
Forgiveness is _____	Church is _____

   Then read Psalm 100 and list the action words.

5. Explain how these two sacred meals dramatize or celebrate significant events to the participants:

   (a) The Passover, Exodus 12

   (b) The Lord's Supper, Luke 22:7–30

6. Read the following passages from the Book of Acts, list them on a sheet of paper, and indicate after each passage referring to "the word" whether it is speaking of (a) word as event, (b) word as message, (c) word as person, (d) word as written. (Note that in some passages "the word" may contain more than one meaning) Acts 2:16; 2:41; 4:31; 6:2, 4; 6:7; 8:4; 10:36, 37; 12:24; 13:44; 13:47; 15:7; 17:11; 19:20.

MEMORY WORK

What do we believe about the Bible?

We believe in the Holy Scriptures, the Old and New Testaments, as the Word of God and the only perfect rule for faith, doctrine, and conduct.

"No prophecy ever came by the impulse of man, but men moved by the Holy Spirit spoke from God" (*2 Peter 1:21*).

Photo by Thomas Medcalf

11

A Book of Life

The Living Word

Sunday	*Psalm 33:1–9* The Creative Word
Monday	*Isaiah 55:6–11* The Powerful Word
Tuesday	*Jeremiah 1:5–12* The Personal Word
Wednesday	*John 1:14* The Word Made Flesh
Thursday	*John 6:60–69* The Word of Life
Friday	*1 Thessalonians 2:1–13* The Word in Life
Saturday	*Isaiah 40:6–8* The Enduring Word

THE PASTOR had just begun to talk with his confirmation class about the Bible. He lifted the Bible in his hands and asked:

"What do you think about this book?"

No one responded.

"Please say what you think," he continued. Then one boy raised his hand and said:

"I think it's dull!"

"Why do you think so?" asked the pastor without being shocked or cutting off the boy's answer.

"That's the way it looks," said the boy.

Do you ever feel like that? Whether the Bible has a black, red, or blue cover, the last part of the first question the church asks of you when you become a member—the part about a rule—does appear rather dull and uninteresting:

> "Do you believe the Bible to be . . . the only perfect rule for faith, doctrine, and conduct?"

The part about the word of God as something moving, alive, speaking and doing things sounds good. But this part about "the only perfect rule" sounds too much like rules and regulations that seem to take all of the fun out of life. "It's so dull!"

Finding Another Word

Perhaps the word "rule" is not the best word to express what the church is most concerned about. After all, we have learned that the Bible is primarily a story. It tells about things that happened. As a story, it needs to be told with excitement and great feeling like it was told by the first witnesses. You can hardly do that with a book of rules.

Some Christians have used the Bible like this, thinking it to be only a book about what's right and wrong, and hitting other people over the head with it for not living up to it, or, at least, those parts they think are important. Some, too, have wanted the Bible to be an answer book for all sorts of questions. They have used it to prove a point or win an argument. But they have missed the point.

Actually, what the church is talking about when it speaks of the Bible as the only perfect rule is not about rules but about authority, a model or pattern or norm against which we can measure ourselves. The prophet Amos spoke about God's truth as a plumb-line (such as a carpenter or bricklayer uses) by which his ancient people were being measured.

What is Authority?

Each of us has many forces and persons of authority that guide our lives and to which we respond in rebellion or obedience. Before going any farther, think of some of the authorities to which you are responsible. The more obvious ones are your parents, teachers, the Constitution of the United States, the laws of the land. Less obvious perhaps are the customs and fads of your friends, the prejudices of your community, and the patterns of conformity which make you a part of the group.

What kind of authority is the Bible? Does it require the acceptance of beliefs as true without the right to question? But is it right to believe something you have never examined for yourself? Are you permitted to approach the Bible with your brains, to ask questions, even to doubt? Or, when the Bible is called in, do you simply have to submit?

Even among Christians who accept the Bible as the final authority, "the only perfect rule for faith, doctrine, and conduct," you often discover two sides—or even three or four—quoting the same Bible at each other, all claiming authority for their position but in violent disagreement. You can also find weird practices supported by the Bible— snake-handling as a sign of faith (from Mark 16) or women keeping silent in church (from 1 Corinthians 11) or other remote passages which become the basis for new sects. Where there is disagreement among Christians, how is it to be settled? By fists, by taking a vote, by debate, by a shouting match, or by starting a new church?

Though Protestants are moving toward a greater consensus than at any time since the Reformation, Lutherans still tend to read the Bible through Luther's eyes, Presbyterians through the eyes of John Calvin, Baptists through Baptist eyes, and Covenanters through Covenant eyes (which may include many different eyes!). Who is right?

Other Authorities

I don't think we'll ever get an answer to that question—here or hereafter. And certainly not by quoting another passage of Scripture. The point is simply this: accepting the authority of the Bible is not as simple as it first sounds. Actually, we accept the Bible's authority because of the presence of other authorities.

You remember, of course, the song you sang in Sunday school as a child:

> Jesus loves me, this I know,
> For the Bible tells me so.

The Bible does tell us so. That's the Good News. But if I believe at all in the love of Christ, it is not just because the Bible tells me so but because that assurance has been tested in real life and found, in one way or another, to be trustworthy. The Bible tells us so, but we accept its final authority because of other authorities like

> home
> church
> pastors
> Sunday-school teachers
> youth counselors
> personal experience
> good, hard thinking
> the Holy Spirit

That doesn't make the Bible less important or less authoritative. It becomes part of a living conversation involving me and everything I know and experience about life. It draws me into its story as a living, thinking, responding partner. So when we read it, we do not ask: Who is right? Or how can I prove my point? Or is it scientifically accurate? Or do I simply have to submit? Rather, we ask:

> Is it true? Does it make sense? Does it speak honestly about the hurts we feel, the wrongs we see in the world we live in?

When you hear the ring of truth in it, then the Bible has a claim upon you that you can't evade, not if you want life at its fullest and best.

Differing Opinions

But how does the Bible exert this kind of authority over us so that we respond to its claim? Christians have differed on this question for centuries. Covenanters don't all agree either. Our church was born in an atmosphere of reverence for the Bible. A question constantly asked in the early days was this: "What do the Scriptures say?" Early Covenanters were nick-named "readers," with something of a tinge of ridicule because they were so diligent in searching the Scriptures. But even then there were sharp disagreements about the Bible. More recently the Covenant Church has been doing some hard thinking about how the authority of the Bible expresses itself. There are at least two points of view, with many shades and variations:

1. The Bible as originally given is the Word of God and is therefore altogether reliable in all its statements regarding history, science, chronology (order of events), and in all points of theology and matters pertaining to conduct (ethics).

2. The Bible has authority in all matters of faith, doctrine, and conduct, but because human cultures change and knowledge grows there are aspects of what the Bible says and counsels men to do that are not binding on people today.

Which of these viewpoints fits most nearly your own?

As Covenanters who hold differing points of view about the Bible, we nevertheless feel that both viewpoints can live together and that no Christian should be excluded from the fellowship because he holds one viewpoint rather than the other. In fact, the church will be stronger because of the presence of genuine concern for the Bible as the Word of God whatever the viewpoint.

You might think of these two ways of regarding the authority of the Bible by drawing a comparison between different ways of looking at mathematics. In method A you approach figures and numbers literally. You learn that 2 plus 2 equals 4. You can even count it out on your fingers, though I recall this was always discouraged. In method B, however, while 2 plus 2 still equals 4 (and where would we be without that kind of reliability?) you do not think as literally as in method A. You think more in terms of the idea, why and how you arrive at the answer. The numbers 2 and 4 have become working concepts.

Responding to Authority

What's more important than how the authority of the Bible is expressed is that we acknowledge its claim upon our lives. But how do we do this? Think of it like this: just as you honor your parents by letting their ideals and attitudes become a part of your life so that their values influence what you think and do (even if you sometimes rebel), so the Bible becomes an authority when we let it influence our lives. Submit? Yes. But we submit as free persons to a claim that wins its own right

　　—to guide us in crucial decisions
　　—to change our minds about some things
　　—to define the goals for which we strive
　　—to shape our style of life
　　—to lead us into the fellowship of the People of God

because of the One speaking. We hear the voice of the Good Shepherd calling us, and because we belong to him and not to another, we must rise up and follow!

Making the Story Our Own

But, I admit, that's not easy. The confirmation student who said that the Bible is dull was really saying, "It's dull for me because I find it so hard to understand." That is the objection many people have to the Bible. Maybe it might help if we came to look at the Bible like this:

> "The Bible is a special delivery letter with your name and address on it." [1]

But if you receive a letter in a language you don't understand, you'll never know what its message is until you set about to translate it or go to someone who knows the language who will translate it for you. In other words, you must not only accept the Bible, you must understand it. This will mean asking at least two questions:

1. What did it mean to those to whom it was first spoken? This means good, hard work, digging into the passage you are reading with the tools of Bible study, like maps and atlases, Bible dictionaries, a concordance, and commentaries.

2. What does it mean today? This means learning to listen, allowing the Bible to search your heart and to guide your prayers. It also means joining other Christians who are eager to discover how the Bible speaks today.

The Bible and You

Do you remember at the beginning of the year we said that this textbook is about you? However you understand

[1] Robert McAfee Brown, *The Bible Speaks To You* (Philadelphia: Westminster Press, 1955), p. 17.

yourself, you are a human being who just now is beginning to discover life—its charm and trouble, its possibilities and problems. Often you stand as a confused spectator before a confused world. But still you are hungry for life. You want to take everything as it is but without the protective wrapper of experience or full maturity. You do not always understand the consequences of one or another action, or where it might lead. But I believe you want to do what's right and that you want some pattern, some rule of measurement, some message, some signpost to follow.

That's the concern which the church also has for you. It wants more than anything that you find the right way. Therefore it asks you:

> "Do you believe the Bible to be the Word of God, the only perfect rule for faith, doctrine, and conduct?"

What the church wants for you is

—a "faith" so strong that it will support a whole life
—a "doctrine" (or faith with a capital "F," meaning the accumulated wisdom of the church in its long history) so pure that no new discovery will blemish it
—"conduct" so dependable that life need have no regrets since it is lived out in obedience to the will of God and the promptings of the Spirit.

So here's the Book. Dull? I hope not, but a book of life!

Prayer

O God, I am here before you reading my Bible. To put it bluntly, I have to tell you there are parts of it that I find confusing and hard to understand. It sometimes takes sheer grit to stick with it. But I thank you that there are some parts of the Bible I do understand, like the stories of things happening and, especially, the stories Jesus told. Help me to keep reading the Bible, even those parts I don't understand now, but more, to act on those parts that I do understand. In Jesus' name. Amen.

Some Things To Do

1. Be prepared to discuss the following questions in class:

   a. What questions would you put to the Bible if you could ask any questions you wanted to?

   b. What questions do you think the Bible puts to those who read it seriously?

2. Look for pictures in *Life* or *Look* of people listening. Bring them to class and display them.

3. Listen to recordings of these great actors reading the Bible:

   Charles Laughton (Decca 8031)
   Charlton Heston (Vanguard 9060–1, Five Books of Moses; Vanguard 9080–1, Life and Passion of our Lord)
   Laurence Olivier (Philips WS-9047)

4. Discuss these two quotations:

   "The scriptural approach to Scripture is thus to regard it as God's written testimony to Himself. When we call the Bible the Word of God, we mean, or should mean, that its message constitutes a single utterance of which God is the author. What Scripture says, He says. When we hear or read Scripture, that which impinges on our mind (whether we realize it or not) is the speech of God Himself."
   —J. I. Packer, *Fundamentalism and the Word of God*
   "That is the true test by which to judge all books [in the Bible], when we see whether they deal with Christ or not, since all the Scriptures show us Christ, and St. Paul will know nothing but Christ. What does not teach Christ is not apostolic even though St. Peter or Paul taught it; again what preaches Christ would be apostolic even though Judas, Annas, Pilate, and Herod did it."
   —Martin Luther

   What, in your opinion, are the strengths and weaknesses of each point of view? Do you think there is a better way of expressing it? If so, how would you do it? Which viewpoint comes nearest to expressing your beliefs about the Bible?

5. Report on one of the following:

a. From the book *For Self-Examination*, by Sören Kierke-gaard, tell what this author says is required in order for the word of God to be a true blessing.

b. From *Life Together*, by Dietrich Bonhoeffer, read Chapter 3, "The Day Alone," and describe the author's suggestions for ordering one's personal life with God.

c. From *Out of My Life and Thought*, by Albert Schweitzer, read Chapter 9, "I Resolve to Become a Jungle Doctor," and tell what factors led him to decide to spend his life in Africa.

d. From *The Screwtape Letters*, by C. S. Lewis, read Chapters 1 and 2 and tell how Screwtape proposes to keep a man from believing in God.

e. From *A Private and Public Faith*, by William String-fellow, read Chapter 4 on "The Fear of God" and tell how the graduate student at the university discovered the Bible.

f. From *The Ring of Truth*, by J. B. Phillips, describe some of his experiences as a translator of the Bible.

g. From *According to Thy Word*, read Chapters 4 and 5 under the section on "The Christian Faith" and describe general revelation and special revelation.

6. Write an essay on the one main idea or theme of the Bible, telling it in story form. Show how this relates to people today.

MEMORY WORK

How is the Word of God to be used?

The Word of God is rightly used when guided by the Holy Spirit we lay hold of its truth, treasure it in our hearts, and practice it in our lives.

"Do your best to present yourself to God as one approved, a workman who has no need to be ashamed, rightly handling the word of truth" (2 *Timothy* 2:15).

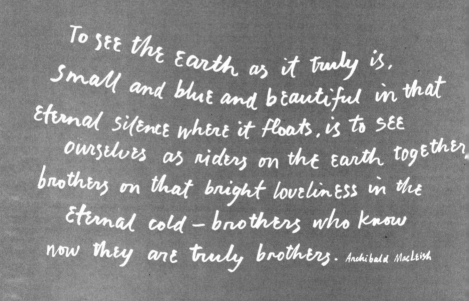

To see the earth as it truly is,
small and blue and beautiful in that
eternal silence where it floats, is to see
ourselves as riders on the earth together,
brothers on that bright loveliness in the
eternal cold — brothers who know
now they are truly brothers. Archibald MacLeish

Poster courtesy of Argus Communications, Chicago

12

The Book about God

In the Beginning, God

Sunday	*Psalm 104:1–9* The Creator
Monday	*Hebrews 11:1–3* By the Word of God
Tuesday	*Job 38:1–7* Where Were You?
Wednesday	*Psalm 8* What Is Man?
Thursday	*Isaiah 40:25–31* Lord of All
Friday	*Colossians 1:15–20* The First-born
Saturday	*Matthew 6:25–34* Trust in God

IT HAD SLIPPED GREG'S MIND that the pastor was giving a test in confirmation on Bible history. He took the test and flunked. When his parents found out about his poor grade and asked him why, he said: "Even if I flunked the test, I have the answers in my heart!" What do you think he meant?

Greg was most likely saying what many Christians in a similar predicament might say—that even though he couldn't give the correct answers to factual statements about the Bible, he was still a believer. Of course, that's not a very good excuse for sloppy thinking about the Bible or the Christian Faith. It certainly doesn't let you off the hook as far as doing your homework is concerned. How far would you get in your math or science class if, after flunking an exam, you said to your teacher, "But I have the answers in my heart"? Your report card would be the answer.

An Important Distinction

But Greg's statement does point up an important difference between faith (with a small "f") and Faith (with a capital "F"). The difference is this:

1. The word "faith" (with a small "f") means the Christian's personal commitment to the God whom he has come to know in Jesus Christ and his attempt to live as a Christian in all of life's relationships.

2. Faith (with a capital letter) means what Christians confess and believe regarding the saving acts of God on which the gospel is based. The church considers it a solemn responsibility to know the Faith, to teach it, and to find—under the guidance of the Holy Spirit— new ways of expressing it so that its message is a live option for people.

As far as faith is concerned, Greg was right. He had the answers in his heart, that is, he had a warm, personal trust in God. Where he was mistaken was in assuming that he could choose between faith and the facts of faith, centering on what he believed in his heart to the exclusion of what he needed to know with his mind. Christianity at its best brings the two together. That is why when you join the People of God the pastor asks:

> "Do you believe the Bible to be the Word of God, the only perfect rule for faith *and* doctrine (or the facts of faith) . . . ?"

The Bible and Creeds

In this question as well as in the following questions you will be asked we shall be concerned with your personal faith in God as well as that which calls forth faith, namely, the proclamation or teaching concerning the saving acts of God.

The church has found it necessary to summarize what it believes in statements of faith called creeds. In fact, it has been forced to do this for at least two reasons:

1) to have an answer to give to others as to who Christians are and what they believe
2) to define the Christian Faith against the background of competing ideas and beliefs.

The Apostles' Creed is one such statement of faith which is helpful even today as a short but true summary of what Christians believe to be most important in their understanding of God. If you are seeking to discover who you are, you will need to learn about the particular heritage in which you have been brought up. This includes, among other things,

—the nation of which you are a citizen
—the community where you live
—the family to which you belong
—the church of which you are a part

The Apostles' Creed represents one historic statement of the church's heritage which you will want to try to understand.

Who Is God?

The first article (or paragraph) of the Apostles' Creed begins:

> "I believe in God the Father Almighty, Maker of heaven and earth. . . ."

That says quite a bit about God, his relation to the world, and to you and me. By contrast, I'm afraid we have often painted a picture of God that resembles

—a spook in the sky
—an old man with a white beard way out there
—someone who's going to get you if you're bad
—the jolly green giant. . . .

How do you think about God? Does your picture of God line up with these popular images or with the first article of the creed?

If you want to find out what the Christian Faith says about God, you must turn to the Bible. In fact, every creed or statement of faith must be judged finally by the Scriptures themselves.

God As Redeemer

If Jewish children were asked: "Who is God?", it probably would never occur to them to say that God is

omnipresent (everywhere)
omnipotent (almighty)
omniscient (all-knowing)
perfect, and so on.

They would be much more specific. They might respond something like this:

> "God is the God of Abraham, Isaac, and Jacob. He is the One who led our forefathers out of the land of bondage. He is the One who has made a covenant with us, thereby making us his people. . . ."

Rather than trying to describe God in terms of what he is, they would describe him in terms of what he does. This would require telling a story of real happenings like

—the exodus
—the conquest
—the exile

These were political and military events involving prophets, judges, and kings. In other words, God was not withdrawn from the human scene, a remote deity someplace beyond the stars; nor was he regarded as the "First Cause" or the "Supreme Being." However great, far-reaching, and over-arching he might be, the Hebrews were sure he was directly at work in the world, right where people were hoping, loving, fearing, hating, struggling, and working. There you would find him at work, making himself known.

One biblical scholar says that to read the Bible correctly one should begin with Exodus (the story of a nation's march to freedom) and then read Genesis (the story of beginnings). That was the order in which the Hebrews came to understand God. He was first of all Redeemer, then Creator. When we read the opening words of the Bible: "In the beginning God created the heavens and the earth," we should remember that we are hearing the confession of a people's faith, the praises of a community that has been called, chosen, and redeemed by God to be his People. Having been set free by God, they could celebrate his power and goodness as the Creator of all things, the Ruler of the universe.

Does this provide us with any clues as to how we as Christians ought to think about God? Can we truly know God as Creator unless we have met him as Redeemer?

God As Creator

But what does it mean to believe in the Creator-God? Again, when we come to the first chapters of Genesis, we must try to think like Hebrews. That is, if we are to hear what these ancient stories of creation are saying we must learn to think like poets and not like twentieth-century scientists.

Let's look again at the first sentence of the Bible: "In the beginning God created the heavens and the earth." Taken as a strict, literal statement, what does this say to you? How do you think it relates to much of what we know about the universe today?

If you attempt to take that statement scientifically, you may run into difficulty. If you read it, however, as a confession of faith which uses a picture-language to express a truth that lies beyond words, then the phrase—and, indeed, the whole story of creation—expresses in a powerful, moving way the faith that

—God stands behind and before our life on this planet
—our life and world are in his hands (another picture-word)
—since God created all things, there is meaning and purpose behind our life and world
—all creation is good

A Conflict Between Science and the Bible?

For many people, the question about the relationship of science and the Bible is a real one. If the Bible is regarded as a textbook on science, or an encyclopedia containing proofs for the existence of God, or answers as to the age of the universe, then some will have problems trying to reconcile what science says with what the Bible says.

If, however, you take the Bible as a road sign pointing you to God, to the meaning and purpose of life, you will be most faithful to what it is—a witness of faith. "By faith we understand that the world was created by the word of God" (Hebrews 11:3).

Science satisfies much of our curiosity as to what things are, how things came to be what they are, how things work, and what principles or laws apply to things. The Christian accepts these findings gratefully, rejoicing that God permits men to think his thoughts after him and to see his work. But the Christian also recognizes that science has its limitations. There is a realm where the exactness of what can be learned in a scientific laboratory or textbook is inadequate. This is the realm where we are more directly concerned with questions of why, what for, and where to.

For my part, I don't think the writer of Genesis was troubled by such questions as the age of the world. If the findings of modern geology had been available to him, he would have been fascinated, no doubt, but not embarrassed. His underlying concern was with the relationship of man to God. That's also the purpose of the Bible; it is a living message pointing us to God. Letting this book be what it is, a testimony of faith to the One in whom the ultimate meanings of our lives are to be found, it is a timeless revelation.

When a Christian says he believes in the biblical stories of creation, he means that he accepts what Christians in all times have meant when they say:

"I believe in God the Father Almighty, Maker of heaven and earth."

In this confession, he acknowledges not only what God has done in ages past but what he is still doing in creating and upholding all that he has made.

Creation and You

But what does all this have to do with you?

Have you ever found a baby bird or animal which you took home and cared for? I once knew a boy who found a baby crow about three weeks old. The bird had fallen from the nest. Bob carefully picked it up and carried it home. Every day he fed it—milk, oatmeal, and earthworms. At last the bird was tamed. Bob was very happy when the crow swooped down and sat on his shoulder when he whistled.

Think what joy man must have felt when he first tamed a dog, or made a fire, or got a boat to float or a wagon to roll. That's the Creator's purpose—to make us his partners, to woo nature, and to rule over the things he has made. For this reason, the first story of creation (Genesis 1:26–28) describes man as made in God's image. This doesn't mean, of course, that God has a human body. What it does mean, however, is that God has made each one of us unique. No one is an exact copy of someone else. He has made us to have dominion over the world. He has put us in charge, saying: "Here is your world, man. Tend the garden, cultivate it, rule over it, love it, celebrate it, be responsible for it, share it with others." We can choose to say Yes or No to God, to accept responsibility or refuse it.

That we can be God's partners in creation is mankind's greatest responsibility but also his greatest joy. The power or law of creation which is at work in a boy taming a bird, or building a model airplane, or learning to play the piano, or paint a picture is the same power which is at work in

—an architect drawing the plans for a building
—the head of a corporation planning a new factory
—a musician composing a piece of music
—a scientist seeking to discover the secret of life
—an archeologist trying to find out the age of the universe
—a politician working for social justice

Does this provide any clues for finding out who you are, what you are called to do, a cause to which you can give yourself? Can you truly know who God is apart from discovering where he is at work in the world today and joining him in his work? Perhaps in this sense Greg was right; God has written the answers in our hearts, in the depths of our being. But finding the answers means a lot of good, hard thinking, studying, and discipline as well as being open to the signals he is giving us as his partners.

Prayer

> Lord, We Know You Love the World That You Created and Redeemed.
>
> We who stand in the world offer ourselves and our society for your blessing and healing.
>
> We confess that we have failed to love as you did. We have been socially unjust, and our society is imperfect, fragmented, and sometimes sick to death.
>
> Teach us your ways in the world and in this life which we share together. Don't let us restrict you to a narrow ghetto labeled "religion" but lead us to worship you in the fulness of life as the lord of politics, economics, and the arts.
>
> Give us light to see true morality, not in narrow legalisms but in sacrifice and open responsibility. Show us how to express our love for you in very specific, human service to other men.
>
> Lord, change our hearts from hearts of stone to hearts of flesh, and let us give thanks to you for all of life.
> —Malcolm Boyd [1]

---

[1] Boyd, *op. cit.*, p. 38.

Some Things To Do

1. In popular songs and in conversation one often hears references to God that make him seem chummy and nice to have around. List some examples and indicate what the Christian understanding of God is.

2. Write out your own translation of Psalm 8, using the language of everyday. (Try to find a copy of *God Is for Real, Man,* by Carl F. Burke, and see how other teenagers translated other Bible passages.)

3. Go to your school or public library and find a copy of *God's Trombones,* by James Weldon Johnson. It is also available in part on a recording by the same name (Decca DL-4345). Read or listen to portions of Haydn's "The Creation," then answer the following questions:

   a. How is God depicted?

   b. What kind of language does the author use?

   c. Which of the two stories of creation from Genesis does he use?

   d. What does it say about man and his reason for being created?

   e. Do you like this way of telling the creation story?

4. Choose one of the following passages of Scripture and make a collage illustrating what the passage says to you about God: Psalm 8, Jeremiah 10:1–16, Matthew 6:25–34. Instead of making a collage you may wish to write a poem, compose a piece of music, or make a painting or drawing.

5. Choose one of these questions for discussion:

   A. *Science and the Bible*

   1. How can a scientist continue to have faith in God?

   2. Do you think a person's understanding of God increases as he learns more about the universe?

   3. In what way is the universe still in the process of being created?

4. If a scientist were able to create human life in a test tube, how would this affect your belief in God?

5. What other sources are there beside the Bible for our knowledge of God?

B. *Faith and Life*

1. What would be changed in our relations with one another if we took seriously the biblical concept that all are created in the image of God? What impact would this have on cliques, race relations, and international affairs?

2. If one believes he is created in the image of God, does this make any difference in his behavior, his attitudes toward himself, and his goal in life? Be specific.

3. Does the story of creation have anything to say to us about capital punishment?

4. If a Christian looks on the world as God's good creation, does this affect his attitude toward material things? If so, how? Does it affect his attitude toward such matters as soil and wild-life conservation, air and water pollution, etc.?

MEMORY WORK

How does God make himself known?

God makes himself known in the works of creation, the events of history, and the voice of conscience, but supremely in Jesus Christ as revealed in Holy Scripture.

"For he has made known to us in all wisdom and insight the mystery of his will, according to his purpose which he set forth in Christ as a plan for the fullness of time, to unite all things in him, things in heaven and things on earth" (*Ephesians 1:9, 10*).

What is God's relationship to man and the world?

God calls the world into being by his Word, upholds it by his power, creates man in his own likeness, and cares for all things according to his wisdom.

"He is before all things, and in him all things hold together" (*Colossians 1:17*).

Strong Son of God, Immortal Love

Strong Son of God, immortal Love,
Whom we, that have not seen Thy face,
By faith, and faith alone, embrace,
Believing where we cannot prove.

Thou seemest human and divine,
The highest, holiest manhood, Thou;
Our wills are ours, we know not how;
Our wills are ours, to make them Thine.

Our little systems have their day;
They have their day and cease to be;
They are but broken lights of Thee,
And Thou, O Lord, art more than they.

Let knowledge grow from more to more,
But more of rev'rence in us dwell;
That mind and soul, according well,
May make one music as before.

—The Hymnal

Unit 4
Confessing the Faith

Learn of Me
by Egon Weiner.
North Park College, Chicago
Photo by Varde

13

Jesus Is Lord!

Confessing the Faith

Sunday	*Deuteronomy 26:5–10* The Lord Set Us Free
Monday	*Mark 8:27–33* You Are the Christ
Tuesday	*Philippians 2:6–11* The Exalted Servant
Wednesday	*1 Corinthians 15:3–6* Of First Importance
Thursday	*Ephesians 4:1–6* The Great Unities
Friday	*1 Timothy 3:14–16* The Mystery of Faith
Saturday	*1 Corinthians 12:1–3* Jesus Is Lord!

"YOU SHALL HAVE DOMINION. . . !" What an inspiring thought! God commissions us to work with him in creating and maintaining the world he has made. But something has gone wrong. Instead of having dominion over the forces of the world, we let the world have dominion over us. All the things that go into this wonderful world God has given us—

> money
> sex
> work
> play
> political power—

things he has given us to use, enjoy, and share with others, we tend to make into little tin gods. Instead of masters, we become slaves.

But not only things have dominion over us. All of us have our own ambitions, dreams, and desires which rule us and make us slaves. These we can also call false gods or idols. Luther says,

"Whatever your heart clings to, that is really your God."

Everyone has something or someone that is more important to him than anything else. To give worth or value to something or somebody—this is what it means to worship.

Good Things Can Become Idols

Let's imagine a husband and wife who give themselves tirelessly for their home and children. In doing so, they are fulfilling God's calling to be his partners. What they do, they do out of love for each other and their children. They work in an honest, responsible way. Now let us suppose the mother desires that her oldest son get a good education, fine grades, and high honors. That's also a part of God's commission. There is only one thing wrong—the son isn't interested. He doesn't like to study. But still mother persists. Why? She says it is for "his own good." What she doesn't say, however (for she scarcely knows it herself), is that she wants a son with high honors so she can talk about "my son. . . ." Something else now has entered the picture. Not only does she have the positive motives of love for her son—"his own good"—but mixed in with these are her own ego and pride—her own good. Instinctively, the son knows this and becomes even more unwilling to study. Of course, mother becomes more and more irritated. She says to her husband, "He surely doesn't take after me!" Now everyone is upset.

It all began so well, with the finest motive: "I want the best for my son." But the "son's best" became an idol. In a similar way, the father and the son had their idols. (What do you think they were?) So it is with everything. Instead of being rulers, we becomes slaves. Not individuals only, but nations, political parties, businesses, industries, unions, and, yes, even churches. Can you think of any other good things that can become idols?

The Earliest Creed

The second question the church puts to you when you become a member asks, in effect, whether or not you are free from slavery to idols and false gods and are therefore free to be what God is calling you to be—his partner:

"Do you confess Jesus Christ as your . . . Lord?"

Does this question sound trite and traditional to you?

When you understand what you are confessing, it can be, in fact, quite bold and exciting, perhaps even dangerous. The earliest confession of Christians was "Jesus is the Messiah." It was the confession Peter made at Caesarea Philippi: "You are the Christ" (Mark 8:29). "Messiah" (or anointed one) is a Hebrew term that was used primarily of kings and sometimes of prophets and priests. It also referred to the one whom many devout Jews were waiting for as the one who would be sent by God to set Israel free from her enemies. For the early Christians this confession of Jesus as the promised Messiah was something quite revolutionary. It meant that Jesus was this active person —the right one in the right place to set things straight, to set men free. Today we might translate the early confession like this: You are the true activist sent from God, the one who takes sides with the underdog, who sets oppressed minorities free, who brings a new order into the old—the administration or rule of Yahweh, God.

The Lordship Of Christ

When Christianity moved out into the Gentile world, the confession was altered slightly: "Jesus is Lord!" In writing to the Romans, Paul states that if one confesses with his lips that "Jesus is Lord" he will be saved (Romans 10:9). He also says that no one is able to say "Jesus is Lord" except through the Holy Spirit (1 Corinthians 12:3). But it is to Paul's credit that he saw in this confession something as radical as Peter saw, namely, a challenge to false gods and idols.

> "For although there may be so-called gods in heaven or on earth—as indeed there are many 'gods' and many 'lords,' yet for us there is one God, the Father, from whom are all things and for whom we exist, and one Lord, Jesus Christ, through whom are all things and through whom we exist"
>
> (1 Corinthians 8:5–6).

In other words, Christians right from the beginning have confessed a rival faith. It is a faith not unlike that of the First Commandment: "You shall have no other gods before me."

But what does this confession "Jesus is Lord" mean?

The Gods Dethroned

The confession celebrates a great victory. Throughout Jesus' earthly life, but especially in his death and resurrection, he entered into conflict with evil, unmasked and conquered it so that men could know themselves as free men, free from the power of idols, free to be what God intended them to be. Paul expressed it like this:

> "On that cross he discarded the cosmic powers and authorities like a garment; he made a public spectacle of them and led them as captives in his triumphal procession"   (Colossians 2:15, *New English Bible*).

You recall the Good News which the early Christians were so eager to announce: "Jesus lives! He died, but he did not stay dead. God raised him up and made him Lord over sin and death, principalities and powers." Because of this victory, the gods and idols have been banished. One young churchman put it like this:

> "Whenever the Christian faith is proclaimed and lived out, gods tumble. The moment the mission built a hospital in Central Africa, gods were fired." [1]

For this reason, when the People of God gather for worship, they are not trying to keep alive a beautiful memory of one who was once their leader; they are celebrating the victory of a living Lord who has all power in heaven and on earth.

Lord Over History

The confession affirms, also, his present lordship over history. When the early Christians said "Jesus is Lord," they were not making a statement about their own personal piety. It was a statement about the universe, and, more particularly, about Caesar.

This faith was difficult to maintain for at least two reasons:

1. There weren't any visible signs of the reign of Christ.

---

[1] Albert H. van den Heuvel, *The Humiliation of the Church* (Philadelphia: Westminster Press, 1966), p. 43.

After all, Caesar still sat on his throne while Palestine lay under the conqueror's heel. Sin, ignorance, disease, and death still thrived, with no signs of being checked. Yet Christians claimed to be living in the reign of Christ and so affirmed: "Jesus is Lord." They believed the whole meaning of history could be scooped up into this one clear cry of faith.

2. Further, you couldn't be politically neutral and make this confession. This, of course, proved to be costly.

Toward the end of the first century, when Christians were increasing in numbers, Roman officials couldn't help but take notice. The new movement constituted a direct threat to Caesar's power. When Christians refused to join in the worship of the emperor by placing a pinch of incense before his altars, they were considered to be disloyal and unpatriotic. For them, Jesus and not Caesar was *kyrios* (kur-e-oss), literally, military commander-in-chief, one who is to be obeyed unconditionally in all areas and relationships of life, including the political. They would declare that Jesus Christ had authority over the whole world. He and not Caesar was the ruler of the universe.

The Confessing Church

Through the centuries the confession "Jesus is Lord" has continued to have special meaning for Christians in times of political upheaval. When Adolf Hitler became more and more inhuman in his policies and claimed more and more authority, many Christians in Germany began to resist. The term "the confessing church" came into common usage as Christians were called upon to decide: Is Hitler or Jesus Lord?

A famous man of letters, Thomas Mann, wrote a preface to a book of sermons by Martin Niemoller, *God Is My Fuehrer*, in which he tried to help American Christians understand the predicament of many German Christians:

"You have chosen, let us suppose, the calling of a theologian, of a minister, of a preacher of the Gospel; inspired by love and faith you have become a pulpit orator, upon whose words hang many thousand simple souls. Politics are alien to you, not at all in your field, for they make up 'the world,' while yours is the realm, as you conceive it, of the spiritual and the eternal. You are a purely religious person, quite; ready to render unto Caesar the things that are Caesar's, but whose real domain is God, Sin, Redemption, Death, and Eternity. Then a rogue with effeminate hands rises up, and with the voice of a malicious snappish cur roars amid great acclaim: 'State and Nation are God, and I am State and Nation. Therefore I am God.' " [2]

What is the Christian to do? He has only two alternatives:

1. Either say "my country right or wrong"
2. Or say, "Jesus is Lord."

If Jesus is Lord, it will mean that

—Caesar is not Lord
—Hitler is not Lord
—President so-and-so is not Lord
—home, neighborhood, school, gang are not Lord
—other people are not Lord.

I hope you begin to see that this confession of faith is not simply a Sunday statement but one that has radical implications for all of life. In the face of social and political pressures, to confess Jesus as Lord is to choose sides openly, even when it means taking a risk. No realm is finally excluded from his rule. He is Lord of all or not Lord at all.

---

[2] Martin Niemoller, *God is My Fuehrer* (New York: Philosophical Library, 1941), p. 4.

Lord Over My Life

In more personal terms, what does this confession mean? When you are asked, upon joining the church, "Do you confess Jesus Christ as your Lord?", the church wants to know if you are really a free person. Your first reaction might be:

> But, of course, I'm free. I can come and go as I please. At school I am free to pick my friends, hang around with anyone I want to. I am free to do as I please, go where I want to, do what I want to do.

Fine. But does it always work out that way? What about some of the pressures of don't, don't, don't, and ya gotta, ya gotta, ya gotta? Are you really free to pick your friends, or did they pick you? How much time do you spend trying to be just like the gang—follow, follow, follow the crowd, or join, join, join the club?

The church wants to know: Have you ever thought about being simply yourself, the person God created you to be and is now calling you to be? To confess Jesus as Lord is to be under One who accepts you as you are, not as a problem or a brat or a kid but as a real person whom he loves and understands. His lordship frees you to be you, the real you.

When the church asks you to confess Jesus as Lord, it also wants to know how prepared you are to commit your life, your ambitions, your talents, and your future to him and what he is calling you to do for him in the world. You acknowledge his lordship

> —whenever, for his sake, you choose service above success in choosing your life-work
> —whenever you go out of the way for someone else
> —whenever you put another's good above our own
> —whenever you give Christ the credit for making things come out right.

But are we able to do this? I think it would be impossible if Jesus were not present in our confession as our constant companion. One of the greatest statements, in my opinion, that Albert Schweitzer ever made came at the conclusion of his moumental study entitled *The Quest of the Historical Jesus,* where he spoke of Jesus as our contemporary.

> "He comes to us as One unknown, without a name, as of old, by the lake-side, He came to those men who knew Him not. He speaks to us the same word: 'Follow thou me!' and sets us to the tasks which He has to fulfill for our time. He commands. And to those who obey Him, whether they be wise or simple, He will reveal Himself in the toils, the conflicts, the sufferings which they shall pass through in His fellowship, and, as an ineffable mystery, they shall learn in their own experience Who He is.[3]

Prayer

> O Lord God, great trouble has come upon me. My cares overwhelm me; I know not where to turn. God, be gracious to me and help me. Give me strength to bear what you send and let not fear rule over me. Provide like a father for those I love. Merciful Father, forgive all my sins against you and against men. I trust your grace and commit my life to your hands. Do with me what you will and what is good for me. Whether I live or die, I am with you and you with me, my God. Lord, I wait for your salvation and for your kingdom. Amen.[4]
>
> —Dietrich Bonhoeffer, martyred
> by the Nazis in World War II

---

[3] Albert Schweitzer, *The Quest of the Historical Jesus* (London: Adam and Charles Black, 1948), p. 401.

[4] *Lutheran Prayer Book,* edited by John Doberstein (Philadelphia: Muhlenberg Press, 1960).

Some Things To Do

1. The Jewish people had their creeds just as we have them today. In these statements of faith, they summed up all God had done for them. Read and report on the following creeds: (a) Deuteronomy 6:20–23, (b) Deuteronomy 26:5–9, (c) Joshua 24:2–13.

2. Write an essay on the various names and titles given to Jesus Christ in the New Testament.

3. After Christ's resurrection, Jesus was known as *Kyrios*, the Lord, with power and glory to save. Explain how Paul speaks of the Lord in these passages: (a) Romans 10:9, (b) Philippians 2:6–11, (c) Colossians 1:15–17.

4. Prepare a creed or statement of faith in your own language which would help a person of your age understand the Christian Faith. (Be sure you read the daily Scripture lessons on "Confessions of Faith" as background.) Be prepared to share your statement with the class for their reactions.

5. Prepare a dramatic sketch on Acts 19:23–41, giving parts to various members of the class. You will want to show how the confession of Jesus Christ as Lord had repercussions in the marketplace.

6. Listen to the recordings of these two alleluias:

   a. Handel's Halleluia Chorus from the *Messiah*

   b. Mozart's Alleluia from the motet *Exsultate Jubilate*

   Your pastor may wish to play these alleluias several times in class, inviting members of the class to join in on some of the parts they feel they can sing. What do you feel in listening to them? What aspect of Christian faith is being affirmed? What does the music tell you about Christ's lordship?

7. You may wish to discuss one or more of the following:

   a. What does the lesson mean by idols, and how does Christ expose men's idols? Be specific.

   b. Why were various people afraid of Jesus? The Pharisees? Herod? The chief priests? Pilate? (See Mark 3:1–6; 6:14–29; 11:27–12:12; Luke 23:1–2.)

c. Do you think that the early Christians' insistence on "Jesus is Lord" in an empire that insisted "Caesar is Lord" was downgrading to the government? (Read Romans 13:3–6a.)

d. How can a Christian best serve his government?

e. What kind of sacrifice may Christ demand if you confess him as Lord in the twentieth century?

f. What do you think it means for a Christian to be a free man?

g. What do you think of the following statement from the best-known scientist of the century, Albert Einstein? Though not a Christian, he wrote of "the confessing church" in Germany as follows:

"Being a lover of freedom, when the revolution came in Germany, I looked to the universities to defend it, knowing that they had always boasted of their devotion to the cause of truth; but, no, the universities immediately were silenced. Then I looked to the great editors of the newspapers whose flaming editorials in days gone by had proclaimed their love of freedom; but they, like the universities, were silenced in a few short wacks . . . . Only the Church stood squarely across the path of Hitler's campaign for suppressing truth. I never had any special interest in the Church before, but now I feel a great affection and admiration because the Church alone has had the courage and persistence to stand for intellectual truth and moral freedom. I am forced thus to confess that what I once despised I now praise unreservedly." [5]

[5] *Time,* Vol. xxxvi, No. 26, Dec. 23, 1940.

MEMORY WORK

Who is Jesus?

Jesus of Nazareth is God's Son, our Savior and Lord, who according to God's promise came into the world to save sinners.

"The saying is sure and worthy of full acceptance, that Christ Jesus came into the world to save sinners. And I am the foremost of sinners" (*1 Timothy 1:15*).

Second Article of the Apostles' Creed

I believe in Jesus Christ his only Son, our Lord; who was conceived by the Holy Spirit, born of the Virgin Mary; suffered under Pontius Pilate, was crucified, dead, and buried; he descended into hades; the third day he rose again from the dead; he ascended into heaven, and sitteth on the right hand of God the Father almighty; from thence he shall come to judge the quick and the dead.

What does this mean?

I believe that Jesus Christ—true God, Son of the Father from eternity, and true man, born of the Virgin Mary—is my Lord.

He has redeemed me, a lost and condemned person, saved me at great cost from sin, death, and the power of the devil— not with silver or gold, but with his holy and precious blood, and his innocent suffering and death.

All this he has done that I may be his own, live under him in his kingdom, and serve him in everlasting righteousness, innocence, and blessedness, just as he is risen from the dead and lives and rules eternally.

This is most certainly true.

Drawing by Neale Murray

14

He
Who Saves

Saving Deeds

Sunday	*Isaiah 52:7–10* Behold Your God
Monday	*Matthew 5:17–20* Prophet of Righteousness
Tuesday	*Mark 12:13–17* Let God be God!
Wednesday	*John 3:16–21* To Save, not Condemn
Thursday	*Hebrews 4:14–16* Our High Priest
Friday	*1 Corinthians 15:20–28* The Lord Reigns
Saturday	*Revelation 19:11–16* King of Kings

HAVE YOU EVER SEEN a copy of the New Testament with the words of Jesus printed in red? Let's tune in on an imaginary conversation between two people who are discussing the purchase of a Bible for a friend:

> How much should it cost?
>> As little as possible, as long as it has what Jesus said in red.
> Why are you so sold on red?
>> 'Cause it's easy to find all the things Jesus said. You know, the familiar sayings, the stories he told, and the Sermon on the Mount . . . .
> Are the things Jesus said more important than the rest?
>> The rest of what?
> The rest of his life. Is what Jesus said more important than what Jesus did?
>> Come again.
> Are parables and stories more important than miracles?
>> What are you getting at?
> Nothing in particular. Just wondering why all the red ink for his speeches when He was really famous for what He did.[1]

The point, of course, is that what Jesus did is just as important as what he said. His life in action is also his word, his proclamation. Apart from what he did we should not be nearly as eager to listen to what he said. Perhaps the solution might be a New Testament that prints the things Jesus did in red. But then we might slight the things he said.

The other part of the second question which one is asked upon joining the church focuses on what Jesus did as Savior, his work for us, even as the question about confessing him as Lord centered on who he is and what God has made him to be:

"Do you confess Jesus Christ as your Savior. . . ?"

---

[1] Herbert Brokering, *Worlds of Youth* (St. Louis: Concordia Publishing House, 1967), pp. 53, 54.

Different Pictures of Christ

The New Testament has many different ways of looking at what Jesus did. You discover such recurring themes as these:

> Christ as teacher
> Christ as healer
> Christ as servant
> Christ as friend
> Christ on the cross
> Christ of Easter

Each of these themes reflects the one great event of Jesus the Christ. Though he is "the same yesterday, today, and forever," Christians in every age find in him that which speaks to the problems and needs they confront at a particular time and place. One great philosopher and theologian, Teilhard de Chardin, speaks of Christ in terms that reflect the scientific concerns of the twentieth century. He came to think of him as "the apex of creation," the One toward whom all creation is moving and in whom all things hold together.

Perhaps at this point it might be well for you to pause a moment and ask yourself some questions.

> What picture of Christ says most to me?
> What best summarizes his meaning for my world?
> How has he helped me?

It would be unfortunate, however, if we should reduce the richness and variety of Christ and his work to one theme. Perhaps there is no single theme large enough to hold all the other themes together. That is why we need the Four Gospels, with Mark's way of looking at Christ along with Matthew's, Luke's, and John's. That is also why we need the witness of Christians from every age who have met him and shared their experiences of him with others.

There is nevertheless an interesting way of speaking of his work which attempts to combine the many different pictures or images which the New Testament conveys of him. For centuries the church has summed up Christ's work for us under three headings:

Prophet
Priest
King

This classification was used by the fathers of the early church, later by the reformers, and it is still being used by Christians. One major problem with this kind of formula, however, is that the terms are drawn from another age in which the prophet, priest, and king were familiar figures. We may have to work hard, therefore, to translate these words into ideas and images that are more familiar to our world today. Or we may even have to search for new images that better express Christ's work for us, not only then but now. For the present we shall hold to the traditional formula.

Christ As Prophet

Have you ever heard someone say something like this?

"I can't accept all these complicated notions that belong to Christianity. Of course, Jesus was a good man and a great teacher. My religion is simple. I try to live up to the Sermon on the Mount. But this business about miracles and creeds is all very confusing, so I let that go."

To help us in our groping and confusion, God sent Jesus to us as the greatest of his prophets. A prophet, we remember, is one who speaks for God, interprets what God is doing and will do in the world, and shows men God's will. The prophet's message was always more important than the prophet himself, which is why the last of the prophets before Christ, John the Baptist, could speak of himself as nothing more than "a voice crying in the wilderness" (Matthew 3:3).

The first Christians saw in Jesus a prophet like no other. He said of himself:

> "I have come to complete the prophets"
> (Matthew 5:17, Phillips).

As messenger of the coming kingdom of God, his battle cry was:

> "The time is fulfilled; the kingdom of God is at hand; repent and believe the gospel"   (Mark 1:15).

Everything he said and did—whether by parables and sermons or by acts of healing and compassion—drove home this central theme:

> The administration of the Lord is at hand. The period of waiting is over. The bad guys are about to be thrown out. God's rule is to begin. Get ready for it.

As the messenger of God's kingdom, Jesus was a revolutionary figure. Today we might call him an agitator, or, at least, an activist who tells it like it is. Certainly his message was far more than an inspiring devotional talk with a nice moral tacked on at the end. On one occasion he interpreted his message with a quotation from the Old Testament, referring to himself as a "stone of offense." His word was like that, a stone lying in the path. While it frequently gave comfort to the troubled, sinful, and despairing, it also tripped people up. For this reason many considered him to be an agitator.

The Kingdom In Your Midst

The first Christians saw Christ the prophet as more than a messenger. He was also the message. Because he is God's word in person, the kingdom comes in him. You see it happening in him. God's will, his love and righteousness, burst into flame as an unquenchable fire wherever he entered. When crowds listened to him, they felt they were being addressed by God himself. When men saw his works, they were also seeing God at work. Because of the fire of his words and deeds he became the center of conflict even though men saw God's love revealed in him. Strangely enough, the most dangerous opposition came from the most deeply religious people, who were filled with longing for the coming of the promised Messiah. One of the most moving pleas any prophet ever made was made by Jesus toward the end of his life:

> "O Jerusalem, Jerusalem, killing the prophets and stoning those who are sent to you! How often would I have gathered your children together as a hen gathers her brood under her wings, and you would not!"
>
> (Matthew 23:37).

Christ As Priest

Just as the first Christians saw Jesus as a prophet like no other—the messenger of God's kingdom but also the message—they saw him also as a priest like no other. In the Old Testament the priest was the one who offered the sacrifices and administered the means whereby sin could be atoned for and thus removed. He acted as a go-between, a mediator between the sinner and God. By offering a sacrifice the priest became the symbol of atonement, bringing the Holy God and sinful man together in peace. Jesus, however, was a priest who offered himself as sacrifice both in his life and in his death.

As prophet, Jesus called men to participate in the kingdom of God, to live out their lives under God's rule. He promised the kingdom to all who were

poor in spirit
meek

> hungry and thirsty for righteousness
> merciful
> peacemakers
> persecuted for righteousness' sake
> ready to turn the left cheek when struck on the right
> ready to give up their last coat
> ready to go two miles if asked to go one

We see it all lived out in Jesus. Fine! But when he begins to say that this is how we participate in his kingdom, we begin to squirm. Despite the fact that we would like to keep religion simple and reduce it to the attempt "to live up to the Sermon on the Mount," we know we are not up to it. It's not the way we want to live, even if we could. We also see what happened to Jesus, who lived it out on a day-to-day basis, how at last he was slandered, beaten, deserted by friends, and executed as a criminal. This is simply a reminder that when confronted by such radical demands we need more than a revolutionary figure. We need a priest, a go-between, or, in more contemporary speech, one who is the innocent, voluntary sufferer—like the medic who dashes onto the field of battle under machine-gun fire and risks his life for another.

God Was in Christ

Christians have always pondered the mystery of Christ's saving work. Early Covenanters discussed the meaning of his sacrifice more than any other question. The message of the cross brought them freedom and peace. They did not see God as a revengeful judge who required the death of Jesus to satisfy his anger but as a loving father who

> "was in Christ reconciling the world to himself"
> (2 Corinthians 5:19).

At the cross, it was God who suffered in order that he might show us his love and receive us back again as his children.

Here is what this message came to mean to one young person:

> "The teen-ager was crying. That weekend she had been with some young people who had been talking with her about Christ and what he meant to them. The lonely, guilt-ridden girl had never heard anything like this before. 'God loves me,' she cried. 'And I thought nobody did!' " [2]

For this purpose Christ the High Priest came as the Suffering Servant, offering himself in sacrifice so that all might know the greatness of God's love.

Christ As King

Kings are almost a thing of the past. Now we speak of presidents, secretaries of state, justices of the Supreme Court. But we can look back to a time when kings were more than figureheads, when they were guardian-figures and rulers. The early Christians saw in Christ a king like no other, the Anointed One sent by God to rule over and defend them. Everything we said in the last chapter in speaking of Jesus as Lord applies to Christ as King. Through the resurrection he has mounted his throne. He is now Lord and King over power-structures, false gods and idols, and the Evil One.

Affirming Christ's kingship, Paul says:

> "He must reign until he has put all enemies under his feet"   (1 Corinthians 15:25).

At present, we cannot see his rule. The evil powers are still at work in the world, creating a lot of havoc. But because Christ is King, these evil powers are "on a leash." While they can still do plenty of damage, Christians believe they are doomed. But there are spots where you can see Christ's

---

[2] William M. Ramsay, *The Meaning of Jesus Christ* (Richmond: CLC, 1964), p. 194.

rule. Christ rules in the hearts of those who love and obey him and in the church that is faithful to him and to his mission. Knowing him as King, Christians live toward the future in hope, knowing that in God's own good time and in his own way the final triumph of his kingdom will surely come.

Our Guardian and Defender

In Shakespeare's famous play, *Henry V*, there is a moving scene which shows us the kind of king Christ is now for his church.

> "On the night before the Battle of Agincourt, the outnumbered English soldiers were huddled in small groups about their campfires, restless with forebodings of the battle to come, and fearful of what might be their fate. Then something remarkable happens. King Henry leaves his royal tent and walks among the men like one of them. He gives a word of encouragement here, a greeting of confidence there. Next day the king who had been one of them gave the command to charge and he himself led the attack. They won the victory because of what the poet calls 'a little touch of Harry in the night.'"[3]

We all know what it means to be afraid. Perhaps you are afraid of what the future holds for you—or maybe it's something at school or home. The night seems dark. But then right into the middle of this night comes Christ the king. He comes as one of us, speaking words of encouragement and hope. He doesn't promise us an easy time. He knows the battle will be hard. But he leads the attack. Because he has already faced the enemy and conquered him, we can follow with confidence wherever he leads. We have nothing to fear. We can face anything that comes with such a King, for he says, "Lo, I am with you always. . . ."

---

[3] William M. Ramsay and John Leith, *The Church a Believing Fellowship* (Richmond: CLC, 1965), p. 41.

Your Response

We have explored one way of bringing the many themes of Christ's work into some kind of unity. He is

Prophet
Priest
King

This, of course, is not the only way. Perhaps it is not even the best way. After all, you can't contain Christ in any formula or definition, however good. New dimensions of his life and work are always being disclosed, for he is still speaking and working. Nevertheless, he is and will always remain the One who comes speaking the word of God, healing the sick, offering friendship to sinners, dying on the cross, and rising to new life. What he began to do and teach he is now able to do and teach in a fuller, freer way because he is alive forevermore.

When the church asks:

"Do you confess Jesus Christ as your Savior and Lord?"

it is not inquiring into your ability to discuss interesting ideas about Christ, much less to prove that he is Savior and Lord. The church is only concerned with your willingness to be open to him, to receive both what he says and what he has done. Perhaps it is only those who hear him say "Follow me" and who stand up and say "Yes" who can really know who he is and what he can do. But it may require sacrifice!

Prayer

And if you permit us to know the many magnificent secrets of science, do not let us forget the one thing necessary; and if you desire to extinguish the vigor of mind or if you let us grow old on earth so that our soul gets weary, one thing there is that can never be forgotten, even if we forget all else, that we are saved by your Son. Amen.

—Sören Kierkegaard (1813–1855),
Danish philosopher and theologian

Some Things To Do

1. Report on the Christian symbols used in your church building and tell how they express various aspects of Christ's work. You may wish to draw these symbols and write an explanation under each one.

2. Make a pictorial study of the various forms of the cross. Your church library or pastor can provide resources to help you.

3. Report on the meaning of the church year—its seasons, colors, themes—and describe how it enables Christians to enter into the continuing life of Jesus Christ as Lord and Savior.

4. Make a mural with several panels showing (a) Christ as Prophet, Priest, and King or (b) how Jesus comes as Man. Lord, Son of God, and Savior.

5. List reasons why Jesus has been compared to Moses and the prophets and tell why he is greater than all of them.

6. Write an essay on the teaching of the atonement as set forth by Dr. P. P. Waldenstrom, one of the early fathers of the Covenant. You will be able to find references in such books as *According to Thy Word, By One Spirit,* and other books available in your church library.

7. Look for the following artists and their paintings of Christ:

a. Holman Hunt and his painting "The Light of the World." Hunt was an English painter of the nineteenth century. Observe in this well-known painting how Christ is dressed. What suggests Christ as Prophet, Priest, and King? What other things impress you in this painting? Does it suggest any Scripture passages or hymns?

b. Georges Rouault, a twentieth-century painter. Some have called him the great Christian painter of this century. Try to find a copy of "Christ Mocked by Soldiers." How do you feel the artist is responding to Christ's sufferings? Do you think he expresses the meaning of Christ for men today?

You may need to go to the public library to complete this assignment. Be sure you look in the book *Christ and the Fine Arts*, by Cynthia Pearl Maus, or in *The Gospel in Art*, by Albert E. Bailey.

8. Be prepared to discuss the following questions:

a. Do you think in an age accustomed to TV stars, astronauts, scientists, and presidents that speaking of Christ as Prophet, Priest, and King sounds rather out-of-touch? How might we describe Christ in terms of our culture today? Are there any modern images that might better express the meaning of Christ for our time?

b. Discuss the following quotation:

I have a dream that one day this nation will rise up and live out the true meaning of its creed: "We hold these truths to be self-evident: that all men are created equal."
I have a dream that one day on the red hills of Georgia the sons of former slaves and the sons of former slaveowners will be able to sit down together at the table of brotherhood. . . .
I have a dream that my four little children will one day live in a nation where they will not be judged by the color of their skin but the content of their character.
—Dr. Martin Luther King, Jr., at the March
on Washington, August 28, 1963.

In what way was Dr. King a prophet? Does his dream correspond in any way to the dream Jesus had of the Kingdom of God?

9. Compose a prayer for someone you know who refuses to accept Christ and his church.

MEMORY WORK

What was the highest expression of the Savior's love for man?

The highest expression of the Savior's love for man was his suffering and death on the cross for the sins of man.

"In this is love, not that we loved God but that he loved us and sent his Son to be the expiation for our sins" (*1 John 4:10*).

What is the significance of Jesus' suffering and death?

By his suffering and death, Jesus has conquered sin, death, and the power of the devil and has made fellowship with God possible for us.

"There is therefore now no condemnation for those who are in Christ Jesus. For the law of the Spirit of life in Christ Jesus has set me free from the law of sin and death" (*Romans 8:1, 2*).

15

Lost
and Found

New Relationships

"SEARCH ME, O GOD, and know my heart; try me and know my thoughts. . . ."

Have you ever heard these words in the pastoral prayer on Sunday morning? Or perhaps you have read them in the Psalms. But have you ever tried to say these words with complete honesty to God? There are those who find such a prayer objectionable.

One objection might sound something like this:

> "I'm not a 'hood.' I don't go around making trouble, beating people up or smashing things. Why this kind of prayer?"

Those who object are usually sincere. "Sin," to them, means breaking the rules. If one manages to keep the rules, then one has a right to feel good about himself. This kind of thinking corresponds to the TV Western with the simple plot of the "good guys" versus the "bad guys." Such persons always come out on the side of the "good guys." Can you think of any parables Jesus told about people whose minds work like this?

Or the objection to such a prayer might sound like this:

> "Of course, I can pray this kind of prayer. After all, we're all in the same boat. We all make mistakes. God knows about these mixed-up lives of ours. He made us this way. So he's bound to understand. It's his business to forgive, isn't it?"

Such persons regard God as benevolent and easygoing—something like an indulgent parent from whom they can accept unlimited tolerance. And sin is something for which they are not responsible. It's a matter of genes (heredity) or geography (environment). Doing the best you can is all that is required.

For others the objection might sound like this:

"Naturally, I'm not perfect, but at least I'm honest about it, and better than most people I know, even those who go to church."

Such persons tend to regard sin as only an illusion of the mind. They would blame the church for taking too gloomy a view of human nature. If people suffer from a guilt-complex, it's the church's fault!

What Is Sin?

We have to admit that the Christian Faith is quite a bit more pessimistic about human nature than any of these points of view seem to indicate. One indication of this is Luther's Explanation to the Second Article that speaks about man as "a lost and condemned person." But the Christian Faith may turn out in the end to be a lot more optimistic about human nature than any of these viewpoints suggest.

The old catechism defines sin like this:

". . . all in word, thought, and deed that is contrary to the will of God."

That takes in quite a bit, doesn't it? But it's a definition that is rather hard to pin down. The key word is in the last phrase. What is "the will of God"? Because this takes some hard thinking we usually take the easy way out by concluding that "the will of God" must surely mean a list of rules. So we end up by thinking of sin as certain bad acts like

cheating on exams
getting drunk
gambling
playing around with sex, and so on

But this is really too easy. Sin is something far more subtle and serious and "the will of God" a lot more demanding.

The catechism answer may become clearer if we try to think of "the will of God" in terms of God's purpose in our relationships. From the stories of creation we discover that God's will for man is

—to live with all people in brotherhood
—to rule over creation
—to live in fellowship with God

Sin, then, is not so much the breaking of rules as the breaking of relationships. God has made each one of us unique. You are one of a kind. You don't need to copy what you see in another. You are free to be completely yourself, to choose your own destiny. That's what the Bible means by saying you are made in "the image of God." You have been created for free and responsible relationships to others, to creation, and to God. But the thing that ought to make us great is the very thing that makes us a problem to ourselves and others. We tend to use our freedom in the wrong way, by saying No to God rather than Yes.

Breaking the Primary Relationship

When we get short-circuited in our relationship with God, there is a power failure in other relationships. That's the meaning of the stories in Genesis that follow the Garden of Eden story—

Cain and Abel
Noah and the ark
the tower of Babel

Man against God starts a chain-reaction that results in

man against man
man against nature
man against group
group against group, etc.

The old catechism calls the consequences of sin "death." This means a lot more than taking your last breath and being deposited in the cemetery. It is something "physical, spiritual, and eternal."

So, you see, sin is a lot more than a series of specific acts. Because the main circuit is broken down, there is power failure all along the line. Here's the way one theologian illustrates it:

> "Getting drunk, for example, is not so much a sin in itself as an indication that something has gone wrong and that life has become profoundly disrupted at its very center. The person who cannot handle his relationships with other people, or who is afraid to face himself as he really is, may get drunk to escape the harsh real world which he feels unequipped to handle into a pleasant make-believe world of his own creation where he is king of all he surveys. His getting drunk, in that case, is only a symptom of a more profound disorder." [1]

Confronting Jesus Christ

Let's try and sharpen this definition still more by looking again at the second question the church asks prospective members:

"Do you confess Jesus Christ as Savior and Lord?"

What makes this question so important is not only what it says about Jesus Christ but what it says about you as a sinner.

You have read many times, I am sure, the story in Genesis about the temptation and fall (Genesis 3). One of the big temptations in reading the story, however, is to think of it merely as a story of how sin entered the world—way back then! It really becomes "our story" only when we meet Jesus Christ. John Calvin said that nobody could ever have

---

[1] Robert McAfee Brown, *The Bible Speaks to You* (Philadelphia: Westminster, 1955), pp. 176, 177.

the courage to see himself as he is if he did not first know that God had loved him and accepted him in Christ.

As we said earlier, you only need to try to do the things Jesus said, and it won't take long before you discover that what the Bible says is literally true—that all men are sinners. This is why Jesus is sometimes called "the Second Adam." We see in him what God intended us to be right from the beginning—free and responsible. But alongside of this "Second Adam" we seem to be like a counterfeit before the genuine article.

Nowhere do we see ourselves more clearly than before his cross. In the presence of Christ crucified we begin to see new depths of sin in ourselves. Here is the right place to begin praying this prayer:

> "Search me, O God, and know my heart; try me and know my thoughts, and see if there be any wicked way in me. . . ."

Through the Eyes of a Child

Imagine a little child hearing the story of the crucifixion for the first time. (It may have happened to you in a similar way.) His mother or perhaps his Sunday-school teacher tells him first about the goodness of this man, Jesus of Nazareth, how he

—preached love of God and neighbor
—healed the sick
—fed the hungry
—befriended the lonely and poor
—opposed evil in every form

The child's eyes grow wide with wonder at such a man. Then the story-teller proceeds to explain how Jesus was hated and at last crucified as a common criminal. The child can't imagine why anyone would want to do such an evil thing to one so kind and good. Explanations don't seem to be of any help. He has to live with this mystery—until later.

Through the Eyes of Maturity

As he grows older, he hears the story again. Now he is able to find things in the story he never realized were there. He remembers hearing how "Jesus died for our sins." He begins to ask: "What sins?" What strikes him now about the story is that the people who put Jesus to death were not monsters but ordinary people very much like himself who, by the standards of their times, were good. The actors in the drama look something like this:

> Pharisees—defending orthodox traditions
> Sadducees—fighting for their right to manage the temple
> Pilate—wanting to maintain his reputation as an efficient ruler
> Soldiers—concerned for maintaining law and order
> People—wanting the release of a popular hero, Barabbas, and also loving excitement

There is only one conclusion he can draw: all of these sins parading as virtues in normally good, respectable people brought the cruel and unjust death of One through whom God had chosen to make himself more fully known.

Now he begins to ask himself: "If I had been in Jerusalem on the day Jesus was crucified, what would I have done about it?", and he lists the possible courses of action:

> —trying to stop it by going to the proper authorities (But where were his friends? What were they doing?)
> —doing nothing
> —doing what everyone else was doing

In the light of the cross, which probes and searches the darker shadows of his life, he discovers that the same sins as those which put Jesus to death can be found in his own heart. The message begins to come through loud and clear: "Look, see what you have done!"

Filling Out the Definition

Comparing our lives with that of Jesus Christ, we discover at least two things about ourselves:

(1) We can break our primary relationship to God by the worship of idols. Do you remember when we said that we are worshipping all the time, giving first place to somebody or something rather than to the God who created and redeemed us? Look back again over the list of the sins of those who helped put Jesus to death. What "good things" tend to become gods in our society today? to the church? to us?

(2) We can also break this primary relationship to God by not caring. One theologian says that apathy is the key form of sin in today's world.[2] The stories of Cain and Abel, Noah and the ark, and the tower of Babel are just as important as the Garden of Eden story, he says, because they symbolize the real nature of man's sin, showing how he wants to look for a way out of the assignment given him by God to live as brother with his fellow man, as partner with God in having dominion over creation. We might add that the story of the cross is possible because good people simply did nothing. The sin of apathy continues the crucifixion wherever you see

—a person in trouble and do nothing to help
—people moving to the suburbs in order to escape responsibility for the city
—people letting more subtle forms of discrimination against the Negro and other minority groups go unchallenged
—allowing others to dictate who you are and how you should live

Even when a person does nothing, his apathy is never a private matter; it always affects somebody else—other per-

[2] Harvey Cox in *God's Revolution and Man's Responsibility* and also *On Not Leaving It to the Snake.*

sons and groups. Indeed, it is a sin against the whole of society.

Healing Broken Relationships

Jesus Christ reveals the nature and scope of our sin in terms of broken relationships between

man and his neighbor
man and creation
man and himself
man and God

but he also sets forth a way whereby broken relationships can be overcome. An ancient hymn expresses it in this way:

A second Adam
To the fight and rescue came.

Paul puts it like this:

"Then as one man's trespass (Adam) led to condemnation for all men, so one man's act of righteousness (the Second Adam, Christ) leads to acquittal and life for all men" (Romans 5:18).

While the cross shows us the sins which brought Jesus to his cruel and unjust death, Jesus did not die as a martyr, as one overcome by hostile powers because he was true to himself. Rather he went into the final, crucial battle with nothing but his faith in the power of love and his trust in God. He offered himself up as a sacrifice so that we might be free from service to false gods and idols, free for restored relationships—which is what Paul means by "life for all men." The Second Adam's act of righteousness was in taking the consequence of our sin and refusing to hold it against us so that our relationship with him might be restored. Now listen to that other part of Luther's Explanation of the Second Article:

"He has redeemed me, a lost and condemned person, saved me at great cost from sin, death, and the power of the devil—not with silver or gold, but with his holy and precious blood and his innocent suffering and death. . . ."

Salvation

This is what the church means when it speaks of salvation. The ancient root of the word "salus" is the word for "health." To be saved means to be restored to health and capable through the power of God's forgiving love to live as persons fully alive and free in all of life's relationships—

> family
> friendships
> community
> school
> daily work
> leisure

Only as we give ourselves to God's loving purpose—what we spoke of earlier as "God's will," not only for us but for the world around us—can we know the real meaning of salvation.

That's part of what the church has in mind when it asks:

> Do you trust yourself to Jesus Christ as Savior, the one who makes people whole?
>
> Do you accept the freedom and new life of restored relationships that God offers?
>
> Will you allow him to be the Lord of all your relationships, and follow him—cost what it may—in serving his will and purpose?

Now perhaps you would like to pray the whole prayer with which we began this chapter:

"Search me, O God, and know my heart; try me and know my thoughts, and see if there be any wicked way in me, and lead me in the way everlasting"
(Psalm 139:23, 24).

Prayer

Almighty God, unto whom all hearts are open, all desires known, and from whom no secrets are hid: Cleanse the thoughts of our hearts by the inspiration of thy Holy Spirit that we may perfectly love thee and worthily magnify thy Holy Name; through Christ our Lord.
—from the Seventh Century

God, we can't con you.
You're on to what we think—
So clean us up.
Then what we say will be square
And we will live on the level.
May Christ help us to do this.
—Paraphrase of the above prayer
written by a kid from the city streets [3]

Some Things To Do

1. Read the Parable of the Prodigal Son (Luke 15:11–24). Your pastor may wish to divide the story into sections and assign each student a part of the story. Take the important words from the section assigned to you. Then from *Life*, *Look* or other magazines cut and paste words and pictures on heavy paper to tell the meaning of these words. Be sure you don't simply tell the story as reported in the New Testament but tell what the story means in terms of your life today.

2. Find stories of people who have either turned away from God altogether or who hurt others by daily selfishness and lack of love. Write your own ending to one of these stories, showing how the persons involved might be helped by the love of God.

[3] Carl F. Burke, *Treat Me Cool, Lord* (New York: Association Press, 1968), p. 80.

3. Read Genesis 3:15 and compare it with Romans 5:17, 18. Write an essay on why Christ is called "the Second Adam."

4. Read Luke 15 (the entire chapter) and write a paragraph on what you think these three stories say about the church —(a) what it is, (b) what it does, (c) what makes it happy, and (d) who belongs in it. (You will have to apply the stories to the church since the church is not directly mentioned in them.)

5. Be prepared to discuss the following:

a. Why can't a man, like the rest of creation, simply be what he is? Why must he seek for the meaning of his humanity?

b. How do the actions of one person affect all the members of society?

c. Is there any sense in which the crucifixion of Jesus continues today? If so, how?

d. What does apathy mean? Do you see any signs of apathy in your community? Do you think it is more sinful to act and make a mistake or to take a "wait-and-see attitude" and do nothing?

e. What does salvation mean in terms of the family, friendships, community, school, daily work, leisure? Be specific.

MEMORY WORK

What is sin?

Sin is our willful refusal or failure to love God, his creation, and our neighbor as ourselves.

"This is the message we have heard from him and proclaim to you, that God is light and in him is no darkness at all. If we say we have fellowship with him while we walk in darkness, we lie and do not live according to the truth" (*1 John 1:5, 6*).

What are the results of sin?

The results of sin are that we hurt others and ourselves, weaken our ability to know and do God's will, and, above all, separate ourselves from him.

"Do not be deceived; God is not mocked, for whatever a man sows, that he will also reap" (*Galatians 6:7*).

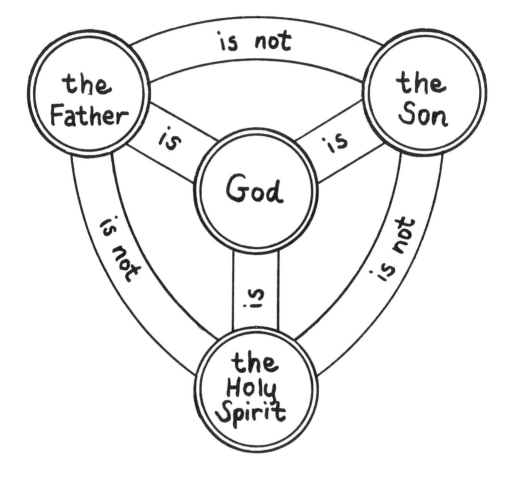

16

The
Strong Name

In This Name

Sunday	*Matthew 3:13–17* Jesus' Baptism
Monday	*Matthew 28:16–20* The Great Commission
Tuesday	*Isaiah 6:1–8* I Saw the Lord
Wednesday	*Romans 11:33–36* Riches of God
Thursday	*Ephesians 2:13–18* Peace with God
Friday	*1 John 4:1–6* The True Confession
Saturday	*2 Corinthians 13:5–14* The Benediction

Do YOU RECALL the story of Robinson Crusoe on his island? At the beginning he thinks he is all alone. Then he begins to discover clues here and there which lead him to suspect that there is someone else on the island. Some of the clues were footprints in the sand—which might have been those of an animal—and the warm remains of a fire. Now he knows without a doubt that there is another human being on the island. Gradually from these clues and the reflections they arouse in him, Robinson begins to form an idea of what his invisible companion might be like. Then one day on the beach he sees this companion coming toward him. A meeting occurs! Now his former impressions—acquired from clues and his own reflections—must be corrected, filled out and enriched. What he had previously imagined is now replaced by personal knowledge. This new knowledge transforms not only his ideas but his whole life because another living person has entered his world.

The Confession of a Mystery

Sometimes young people are disturbed because they think the attitude of the church toward other religions is: "We are right, and all the other religions are wrong." They feel that this is a kind of arrogance that is far removed from the Good News the church should proclaim.

The fact of the matter is that all religions, even the strangest brands, contain some hints of truth. What the church declares is the Good News that God has not remained content to let us seek him, nor has he left us to try to figure things out for ourselves. The Good News declared by the church is that God has taken the initiative of coming to us in the person of Jesus Christ and seeking us out.

Behind the second question:

"Do you confess Jesus Christ as your Savior and Lord?"

there is a great mystery which has puzzled Christians throughout the centuries. (Mystery is that reality which cannot be grasped by understanding but is an object of faith.) The best minds of the church have wrestled long and hard over the mystery of the living God who refuses to dwell in lonely isolation but comes forth into the world. Another name for this mystery is the Holy Trinity, or the mystery of the Father, the Son, and the Spirit moving out toward the world, toward you and me. Thus, when we say Yes to this second question, we are in fact confessing the mystery about which we often sing:

"God in three persons, blessed Trinity!"

What the Bible Says

The Bible, of course, does not use the word "Trinity" at all to speak about this mystery of God-in-action. The word doesn't appear in Christian teaching until the second century. You might conclude, therefore, that it is not really very important or that it has little meaning for Christians today. However, that would be to deny the witness of Christians in every age, including the earliest Christians.

While you find no doctrine of the Trinity in the Bible, the idea is certainly there. Look, for example, at the way Paul ends a letter to the Corinthians:

The grace of the Lord Jesus Christ, and the love of God, and the fellowship of the Holy Spirit be with you all.
(2 Corinthians 13:14)

If you hadn't heard these words before, what would you make of them? You would probably ask: What goes here? Is Paul referring to one God or to three gods? Does he mean that God, Christ, and the Holy Spirit are different or the same? How can three be one? Is this one of those awkward problems of math?

In spite of all the problems which our minds find with the idea, the fact remains that the earliest Christians spoke of God in three different ways. The idea is solidly anchored in the New Testament. But why this confusing way of speaking about God?

The Witness of Christian Experience

(1) The doctrine of the Trinity arose because it was the only acceptable explanation of what Christians had experienced.

The earliest Christians were Jews and strict believers in one God. They knew the words of the Shema: "God is one" and believed it with all their hearts. That conviction could not be shaken. But after the resurrection of Jesus it wasn't that simple. When they met for

—the apostles' teaching
—fellowship
—breaking of bread
—prayers

they found themselves praising and thanking God for what he had done for them in Christ. Therefore, they worshipped God through Christ. They also called Jesus Lord, for they could not call him less. Yet their new way of worshiping did not make them forget the God whom they had worshipped previously. It was of the same piece. God, as they had come to know him through Christ, was one with the Creator and righteous God of the Old Testament. He had done a new and different thing in Christ. "God was in Christ" working out his purpose for the world.

But that was not all. The early Christians had the experience of being directed and sustained by the power of God living and working within their own hearts and lives, and within the whole fellowship of the church. There was a presence in their midst, enabling them to do things they had never dreamed of doing before

—like facing their enemies with love
—like risking their lives for Jesus' sake
—like going everywhere preaching the Good News

This sense of God's living and working within them, using their poor hands and lips and lives, they called "Holy Spirit." They remembered Jesus' words:

> I will pray the Father, and he will give another Counselor
> to be with you for ever, even the Spirit of truth . . .
> (John 14:16)
> If a man loves me, he will keep my word, and my Father
> will love him, and we will come to him and make our
> homes with him.   (John 14:23).
> I have yet many things to say to you, but you cannot bear
> them now. When the Spirit of truth comes, he will guide
> you into all the truth . . .   (John 16:12)

Experience of God came first. The doctrine followed later as a way of trying to account for what Christians in general have found to be true in God's gracious dealings with them.

The Greatness of God

(2) The doctrine of the Trinity remains important as a way of having Christians bear witness to the greatness of God.

Admittedly, to try to squeeze God into a formula is impossible. God is complete in himself, so complete that no formula can begin to describe what he is. But because of what Christians have experienced of his greatness and power and of his love and forgiveness they have tried to put into words something too great for human minds to comprehend, the mystery of God himself. The doctrine of the Trinity represents such an attempt:

"God in three persons, blessed Trinity."

Does this mean that Christians believe in three gods? It almost sounds that way. But the church has always turned thumbs down on any such suggestion. Perhaps the key word is "persons." Today the word "person" refers to a single individual. The word originally used to describe the Trinity was the Latin word *"persona,"* which had at least two meanings:

(a) the mask worn by an actor in playing different parts

(b) the role an actor played in a drama

Instead of the idea of three distinct or separate individuals comprising the Godhead, it makes a lot more sense to speak of the "persons" of God as the ways God makes himself known to men. That's what the church is trying to say: God is continually related to us and our world as

—Creator
—Redeemer
—Sanctifier

God in these terms is often spoken of as the "Triune God," literally, three in one.

Illustrations

Confronted by the mystery of God's different ways of making himself known, yet bound to the conviction of the oneness of God, the church has worked hard to find ways of illustrating what it means by the Trinity. Here are just a few attempts:

—it is like a man who can be at the same time a son, brother, and father . . .
—it is like water existing in three different forms as liquid, ice and steam . . .
—it is like the sun giving off rays of light, heat, and energy . . .
—it is like a book as conceived in the author's mind, written down, and then read . . .
—it is like being a thinking, willing, and doing person yet one . . . and so on.

But God, of course, goes beyond words and ways of speaking of him. The word "mystery" is very appropriate here, for in the end we can only say:

O the depth of the riches and wisdom and knowledge of God! How unsearchable are his judgments and how inscrutible are his ways! . . . For from him and through him and to him are all things. To him be glory forever. Amen.   (Romans 11:33, 36)

The Mission of God

(3) The doctrine of the Trinity is important also as the best way Christians know of speaking about God's mission in the world.

From what we have just said, you might be tempted to conclude that to speak of God as the Holy Trinity is to waste time in meaningless talk, with little concern about the real world in which we live. Absolutely not! The church can speak about the Trinity only because God is very much involved in this world. Someone has said that the doctrine of the Trinity is simply a way of speaking about God as a "missionary God" who created the world for a purpose and never gave up on it.

That's exciting! It says that God is very much involved with the world. You might try thinking of the Trinity like this:

—The Father is God in his freedom, seeking to enlist us as his partners in making the world one people, one family bound together in mutual love and service.
—The Son is God moving out to us in Christ, breaking the silence, overcoming our hates and hostilities and making it possible for us to live together as one people.
—The Holy Spirit is God pouring power and love into his people, continuing his work in the world, creating and sustaining his world.

But you ask: What does this have to do with mc?

The Trinity and You

We said earlier that we are involved in trying to find out who we are. But it isn't long before we discover that this is not easy. We are all pretty complicated. One Christian who thought long and hard about this question came to this conclusion:

> Selves cannot be discovered as America was found by Columbus, by sailing in the direction of a secret and a guess; this new continent must come to us or remain unknown.[1]

Again, it's like Robinson Crusoe, alone on his island, with plenty of clues but uncertain and fearful about what to expect until his unseen companion comes forth to meet him. We can know ourselves only as those called, sought out, and loved by God. Warm, human, friendly, and full of the love stronger than death—that's how God shows himself in the Trinity. That's how we know ourselves.

If we are not to miss the real purpose of our lives, however, we must follow this one step farther, by asking, "How does he show himself to me?" God always steps out of words and symbols and pictures to embody himself in people, especially the needy ones of earth. He is saying to us: "Here, look for me here . . . in the hungry, sick, imprisoned:

> But if any one has the world's goods and sees his brother in need, yet closes his heart against him, how does God's love abide in him? Little children let us not love in word or speech but in deed and in truth.   (1 John 3:17,18)

The mystery of the Triune God is not a mystery of his dwelling in some far-off, celestial palace but God involved

---

[1] *The Meaning of Revelation,* H. Richard Niebuhr, Macmillan, New York, 1946, p. 145.

in the depths, in the mystery of fellowship, of giving and receiving, of outpouring and fathering up.

Does this say anything to "the Robinson Crusoe" in you, looking for a real though unseen companion?

Prayer

O gracious and holy Father, give me
Wisdom to perceive you;
Intelligence to understand you;
Diligence to seek you;
Patience to wait for you;
Eyes to behold you;
A heart to meditate upon you;
And a life to proclaim you;
    Through the power of the Spirit of Jesus Christ our Lord. Amen.

—Prayer of St. Benedict,
a monk who reformed monasticism

Some Things To Do

1. Complete the following sentences and discuss them with the class:

   Yahweh helped the Jewish people by . . .

   Christ helped people during his earthly life by . . .

   Christ and His Spirit now help us by . . .

2. Write an essay on what Jesus revealed about the Three Persons of the Trinity.

3. Draw symbols used in Christian art to represent the Trinity. (If there are any symbols of the Trinity in your church, you may wish to draw and explain these.) Display these symbols in class.

4. Make a careful study of your Sunday morning service of worship for ways in which the church's faith in the Trinity is expressed. On what other special occasions does the church confess its faith in Father, Son, and Holy Spirit?

5. Be prepared to discuss one of the following:

a. Why do you think the Second Article of the Apostles' Creed has so little to say about the earthly life of Jesus?

b. How can we discover the Holy Spirit or God-at-work in the world today?

c. One theologian has said: "The reason why Christians know so little of the Holy Spirit today is that they have never attempted to witness to the Gospel." What do you think of that?

MEMORY WORK

What does it mean to believe in the Trinity?

To believe in the Trinity is to confess that God is one, and that he continually and personally makes himself known to us as Father, Son, and Holy Spirit.

"The grace of the Lord Jesus Christ and the love of God and the fellowship of the Holy Spirit be with you all" (2 *Corinthians 13:14*).

Third Article of the Apostles' Creed

I believe in the Holy Spirit; the holy Christian church, the communion of saints; the forgiveness of sins; the resurrection of the body; and the life everlasting. Amen.

What does this mean?

I believe that I cannot by my own understanding or effort believe in Jesus Christ my Lord, or come to him. But the Holy Spirit has called me through the gospel, enlightened me with his gifts, and sanctified and kept me in true faith.

In the same way he calls, gathers, enlightens, and sanctifies the whole Christian church on earth, and keeps it united with Jesus Christ in the one true faith.

In this Christian church day after day he fully forgives my sins and the sins of all believers.

On the last day he will raise me and all the dead and give me and all believers in Christ eternal life.

This is most certainly true.

O Master, Let Me Walk with Thee

O Master, let me walk with Thee
In lowly paths of service free;
Tell me Thy secret; help me bear
The strain of toil, the fret of care.

Help me the slow of heart to move
By some clear, winning word of love;
Teach me the wayward feet to stay
And guide them in the homeward way.

Teach me Thy patience! still with Thee
In closer, dearer company,
In work that keeps faith sweet and strong,
In trust that triumphs over wrong.

In hope that sends a shining ray
Far down the future's broad'ning way,
In peace that only Thou canst give,
With Thee, O Master, let me live. Amen.

—The Hymnal

Unit 5
The Way of Discipleship

Amish buggy near Youngstown, Ohio

17

A New Style of Life

.

A New Look

DID YOU EVER DREAM about being a great baseball player, or pole-vaulter, or ballet dancer, or concert pianist? My dreams as a boy to be a great baseball player were nourished by frequent visits to the local stadium, where I watched the hometown team play. I saw some great players, and my favorite pitcher became my model. At times I would dream I could pitch like him. Now I was on the mound—the stretch, the wind-up, the pitch. "Strike!" Now the change of pace—the fast ball, or the knuckle-ball, or the sliding curve. "Strike three! You're out!" The great pitcher had style. I wanted to be like him.

Back at the vacant lot, I played on the neighborhood team. Now the dream became the real thing. I would attempt to re-create the style of my model. In my imagination the grandstands were packed with cheering fans. Now the stretch, the wind-up, and the pitch. Whizz! Right over the head of the catcher! But even the failures didn't discourage me. I knew it could be done. Even when my pitching arm didn't respond as I wanted it to, I found confidence in my model. He had style. Perhaps with more practice I could be like him.

What Is Style?

Actually, almost everything we do has a certain style to it. The word is used by the social sciences to mean the special attitude that a person brings to what he does in the little and big events of every day. We commonly use the word with reference to such things as

    clothes
    music
    art
    hair
    cars
    writing
    etc.

We can also use the word with reference to groups. For example, your family has its own style, which is expressed by such things as

—pizza on Saturday nights
—camping trips in the summer
—going to church together on Sunday morning
—celebrating birthdays in a special way

The style or styles you choose, whether as an individual or as a group, determine who you are and what makes you special and different from everyone else.

The Style of the People of God

The People of God also have style, not simply one style but many. That is, they have a distinctive way of living and acting that marks them off from the rest of society. When you join the People of God, you are asked this question:

> "Do you purpose to remain steadfast in the faith unto the end, and as a true follower of Jesus Christ to walk in newness of life?

The first disciples of Jesus had style. How would you describe what made them different from other people?

—a certain garb?
—a special lingo?
—a strange set of beliefs?
—a cut of the beard?

Probably not! For the Twelve, being disciples meant leaving fishing boats and nets, tax tables and homes for the sake of following Jesus, going wherever he went, doing the things he did, and even sharing his fate. Stop for a moment and read a passage from your daily Bible readings (Matthew 16:13–25) and check it out for yourself.

In every period of Church history since, there have emerged certain distinctive patterns or life-styles which the People of God have adopted to make clear how they are different. These styles have been needed for the particular situation in which the church has found itself. Looking back over the story of the People of God, you might be prepared to discuss in class the life-styles of such groups as

Monastics	Puritans
Franciscans	Methodists
Dominicans	Mennonites
Jesuits	Amish
Lutherans	Pentecostals
Anabaptists	
Pietists	

How were these groups alike? different?

The Style of Covenanters

Covenanters, who are heirs of the early Pietists, have also had their style of living the Christian life. We believe that a living faith in Christ will express itself in a special kind of life which bears such marks as

devotion to Christ
reading of the Bible
personal witness
joy
concern for others

In earlier times, this concern for a new kind of life often came out in a summons to break with the world at certain points. No one ever wrote the rules down, for then they were plain enough for anyone to see: A Christian shouldn't smoke or drink or dance or go to the movies or play cards, etc. To live the life of faith one had to keep himself unstained from the world and maintain a steady gaze on the heavenly Kingdom. Unfortunately, the message that came through the loudest seemed to stress what Christians shouldn't do rather than what they were called to do, namely, to live all of one's life for the glory of God.

If we tend to look more critically at taboos than early Covenanters did, we should remember that while there are dangers in making the style of a Christian a matter of rules (mostly things you shouldn't do), God's People are nevertheless called to live a new and different life. It still means breaking with the world at certain points, but it is always for the sake of something much more positive: to be God's People in the midst of the world and for the sake of the world.

In a world like ours, torn by racial injustice, by the violence of war and the struggle for peace, and by revolutionary changes in standards, we must ask the question positively: How can we live the Christian life in the world today? Is there a distinctive style of life for me as a student? as a citizen? as an employee? as a member of the People of God?

Conformed to Christ

Dietrich Bonhoeffer, the German pastor who became a Christian martyr during the last days of Hitler's regime in Germany, had a lot of time as a prisoner to think about such questions. He had chosen a style of life that had serious consequences. Following his convictions, he called the People of God in his country away from any attempt to withdraw from the world and summoned them to commit themselves to serving God in the world. The Christian style of life involved learning to live a holy life in the midst of the world, for it is the world God is acting to redeem.

For Bonhoeffer, the only authentic life-style was the one given Jesus Christ. The word he used to describe the life-style of the Christian was "conformation." That is, our calling both as persons and as God's People is to be conformed to Jesus Christ—to be made in the likeness of him who was made man, was crucified, and who rose again.

Just as I had my baseball pitcher as my star and model, so for the Christian, Jesus is the Star and Model, the pattern for a life-style.

This does not mean that as Christians we must try to copy Jesus in all his words and acts. That would be impossible. Bonhoeffer knew that only too well. But we should let his teachings, his mind and spirit shape who we are and what we do. Like him, we should seek to respond in every new situation to the will of God as we see it in Jesus. But let's take it in slow motion.

He Was Made Man

Just as God could not remain aloof from the world but came down to this planet and became a real human being like you and me, so we are called to be fully human; as another theologian put it, "to make and to keep life human."

What was the most distinctive thing about Jesus' life as a man? You might find it hard to settle on one mark of distinction, for there were many. Here is a partial list of things that characterized him as a man:

—a man about his Father's business
—a man who was poor
—a man who had compassion for the needy
—a man of prayer
—a man of courage and strength
—a man who was controversial

But if you had to settle for one distinguishing mark in his life-style, what would it be? You probably would get around to saying it was *his love and concern for people.*

Taking this as a clue for our life-style means that we take our place in the world for the purpose of making known through our daily life and witness the love of God for all men. In so doing, we discover who we are and what makes us special as God's People.

He Was Crucified

Just as Jesus risked his life in death for the sake of the world, so we are called to risk something for the love of God and people. Of course, we are not the world's savior; we can only witness to Jesus as the Savior. But such a witness is most convincing when, like our Lord, we have the courage to live our lives where the action is, where people are hurting the most.

To risk something might mean such acts of courage as

—speaking up for your faith when it would be safer to remain silent

—caring about the needs of people when it would be easier to do nothing

—breaking the customary way of doing things because conscience won't let you continue in some stupidity or injustice

—striking out in some new direction when it might require some costly sacrifice

—breaking down some barrier between races or groups when doing so might mean hostility

—loving one's enemies.

When asked to comment on how danger and suffering had affected his thinking, the late Dr. Martin Luther King, Jr., said:

> "Due to my involvement in the struggle for the freedom of my people, I have known very few quiet days in the last few years. I have been arrested five times and put in Alabama jails. My home has been bombed twice. A day seldom passes that my family and I are not the recipients of threats of death. I have been the victim of a near-fatal stabbing. So in a real sense I have been battered by the storms of persecution. I must admit that at times I have felt that I could no longer bear such a heavy burden, and have been tempted to retreat to a more quiet and serene life. But every time such a temptation appeared, something came to strengthen and sustain my determination.

I have learned now that the Master's burden is light precisely when we take his yoke upon us. . . .

"There are some who still find the cross a stumbling block, and others consider it foolishness, but I am more convinced than ever before that it is the power of God unto social and individual salvation. So like the Apostle Paul I can now humbly yet proudly say, 'I bear in my body the marks of the Lord Jesus. . . .'" [1]

Just as the style of life of early Christians included risk and the threat of suffering and death, so the People of God today are beginning to discover that to take part in the suffering and injustices of other people means living a risky life. In fact, it may be risky in certain congregations where the church is not always the supporting, caring community it is called to be. But then we need to pray for "the same sort of love that Christ gave to the church when he sacrificed himself for her" (Ephesians 5:25, Phillips).

He Rose Again

When we study the meaning of baptism, we shall learn more about what the death and resurrection of Jesus Christ mean for the People of God. For now, let's simply say that just as Jesus was raised from death on Easter Day, so we who share his death are continually being brought to new life. Therefore, the life-style of the Christian in today's world is one of *hilaritas* (a Latin word meaning superabundant joy).

Hilaritas is
—the joy of feeling we are being what we were meant to be
—the joy of affirming the selfhood of others—their right to be and to make decisions
—the joy of confidence in one's own work
—the joy that comes when we are able to rise above defeat
—the joy of celebrating life as good.

---

[1] *The Christian Century,* April 27, 1960, "Suffering and Faith."

The Apostle Paul was a man who knew the power of the resurrection and the gift of *hilaritas*. Listen to how he puts it:

> "We are treated as imposters, and yet are true; as unknown, and yet well known; as dying, and behold we live; as punished, and yet not killed; as sorrowful, yet always rejoicing; as poor, yet making many rich; as having nothing, and yet possessing everything."
>
> (2 Corinthians 3:8–10)

Christ in You

How can this style of life become ours? When you join the People of God, the church wants you to be prepared for the long haul of Christian living and asks, therefore, whether you "purpose to remain steadfast in the faith unto the end." The church knows that when you say "I want to live for Christ" it doesn't mean that you have arrived. In this world you will never really make the goal. Like the boy with the dream of copying the style of his favorite baseball player, you will often fall flat on your face. You don't become what you want to be overnight. It takes a lot of training and discipline. So the church wants you to be prepared for a life of struggle and a life of decisions—hard decisions.

But you have a lot going for you. If you choose to follow Christ, you have his help. Do you recall those startling words in Galatians 2:20 ". . . it is no longer I who live, but Christ who lives in me . . . ."? When you make the promise "to remain steadfast in the faith unto the end, and as a true follower of Jesus Christ to walk in newness of life," you are saying you want Christ to take over your life. The "selfish you" must give way to the spirit of Christ. He becomes not only the model or pattern but the power for a new style of life which waits to be discovered by you as a unique thing, something special just for you.

Prayer

Lord, make me an instrument of Your Peace.
Where there is hatred, let me sow love;
Where there is injury, pardon;
Where there is doubt, faith;
Where there is despair, hope;
Where there is darkness, light;
And where there is sickness, joy.
O Divine Master, grant that I may not
So much seek to be consoled as to console;
To be understood as to understand;
To be loved as to love;
For it is in giving that we receive;
It is in pardoning that we are pardoned;
And it is in dying
That we are born to eternal life. Amen.
—Francis of Assisi

Some Things To Do

1. Read Colossians 3:1 to 4:5. (If available, read it from a
modern version, preferably Clarence Jordan's *The Cotton
Patch Version of Paul's Epistles*.) Make a list of vices and
virtues in this passage. Then write down your responses to
these questions: Would you add or subtract anything from
these lists? What is the great virtue to be put first? Why?
Why are certain commands given to family groups? To
young people? Do you agree or disagree?

2. Read the following excerpts from the prison letters of
Dietrich Bonhoeffer and explain in your own words what
you think he means.

Man is challenged to participate in the sufferings of God
at the hands of a godless world. He must therefore plunge
himself into the life of a godless world, without attempting
to gloss over its ungodliness with a veneer of religion or
trying to transfigure it. He must live a wordly life and so
participate in the suffering of God. He may live a worldly
life as one emancipated from all false religions and obligations. To be a Christian does not mean to be religious in a
particular way, to cultivate some particular form of asceti-
cism (as a sinner, a penitent or a saint), but to be a man.

It is not some religious act which makes a Christian what he is, but participation in the suffering of God in the life of the world.[2]

July 18, 1944

Later I discovered and am still discovering up to this very moment that it is only by living completely in this world that one learns to believe. One must abandon every attempt to make something of oneself, whether it be a saint, a converted sinner, a churchman (the priestly type, so called!), a righteous man or an unrighteous one, a sick man or a healthy one. This is what I mean by worldliness—taking life in one's stride, with all its duties and problems, its successes and failures, its experiences and helplessness. It is in such a life that we throw ourselves utterly in the arms of God and participate in his sufferings in the world and watch with Christ in Gethsemane. That is faith, that is *metanoia* [Greek word for repentance], and that is what makes a man and a Christian.[3]

July 21, 1944

3. At the end of Chapter 8 there is a list of several great Christians. Select one of these men and describe his lifestyle. Or you may wish to consider the groups listed earlier in this chapter and describe the life-style of one of these groups.

4. Be prepared to discuss the following real life situations:

a. In a local junior high school paper this incident was reported: "After last week's high school basketball game, an incident at a local restaurant was reported to the school office. When the manager was contacted, he confirmed the fact that junior and senior high students had created a serious problem in the restaurant. Most of the high school young people had dates, so the most serious problems were with the younger students. The restaurant was overcrowded, which probably added to the confusion. However, the manager complained about the youngsters moving from table to table, shouting, throwing straws and menus, smashing candy at the checkout counter, and even sitting on the counter top. Adults that were there at the time stated that the cashier was crying and the cook and a waitress threatened to quit on the spot."

---

[2] Dietrich Bonhoeffer, *Prisoner for God* (Macmillan Co., 1954), p. 166.
[3] *Ibid.*, p. 169.

Now complete the following: If I had been at that restaurant during the disturbance, I would have. . . .

b. A junior high school had formerly admitted only white students. Now black boys and girls were being enrolled too. A popular thing in that city and in that school was to make fun of these new students and call them names. Put yourself in that situation and describe what it might mean to follow Jesus under such circumstances.

5. Try sampling some adult opinions in your congregation on the question: How is a Christian different from others? Be sure to press the point of what the difference is and how it affects others. Then summarize by stating your opinion.

6. Write an essay on the style of Christian life you observe in your congregation and how it has tended to shape your lifestyle. You might include in this how you are expected to dress, how you are to relate to other groups and other activities, how you are to act toward each other, and how you are to work in the community and the world.

7. Discuss certain specific risks a Christian or a congregation might have to take in order to be fully obedient to Christ.

MEMORY WORK

What is the significance of Jesus' resurrection?

The resurrection of Jesus Christ from the dead is the assurance that he is Lord of life and death, and the first fruits of a new creation.

"But thanks be to God, who gives us the victory through our Lord Jesus Christ" (*1 Corinthians 15:57*).

What is justification?

Justification is an act of God in Christ by which he forgives us our sins and accepts us as righteous.

"Therefore, since we are justified by faith, we have peace with God through our Lord Jesus Christ" (*Romans 1:5*).

18

Respect for Persons

I-Thou-We

Do YOU RECALL where you sat last week in confirmation class? It was probably where you sat the week before. In fact, after the first day or two where you and the other members of the class sat was just as predictable as if seats had been assigned.

If your class is typical, there is probably a "demilitarized zone" between two groups. The boys sit on one side and the girls on the other. As a class, you organized yourselves according to sex.

Your Sex

At the outset we asked you to think about the question: Who am I? One of the most obvious and yet significant parts of the answer to that question is:

> I am a girl, or
> I am a boy.

Your sex was one of the most important factors in determining how you were treated as a child

—what toys were purchased for you
—what games you played
—what activities brought reward or punishment
—how you were dressed

If your sex was important when you were a child, it is even more so now that you are a teenager. You have perhaps never been as aware of your sexuality as you are now (that is, what makes you different physically and emotionally from the opposite sex). In one way or another, many of the hurts you feel, the things you worry over, the fights you have with your parents or other kids happen because you are trying to discover who you are in relation to your sex.

Your Body

You are also becoming increasingly aware of your body and its development. You may be discovering that your clothes don't fit, that your best friend is a whole head taller than you, or that your feet don't respond the way you want them to. Size, shape, and signs of developing maturity have suddenly become important.

Your Feelings

But more than bodies change. Your feelings change too. In fact, this may be a time when your feelings seem to get all mixed up.

> *For girls:* One moment you may be playing touch or tackle football and the next sitting before a mirror brushing your hair and putting on makeup.
> *For boys:* One moment you like to be noticed by girls and the next be annoyed that girls show interest in you. You may want to return to activities that clearly distinguish you as a boy.
> *For both:* You probably have brand new feelings that two or three years ago you laughed at in others.

Among the entries in the diary of Anne Frank there is the following statement:

> I saw my face in the mirror and it looks quite different. My eyes look so clear and deep, my cheeks are pink— which they haven't been for weeks—my mouth is much softer; I look as if I am happy, and yet there is something so sad in my expression and my smile slips away from my lips as soon as it has come. I am not happy, because I might know that Peter's (her secret boyfriend) thoughts are not with me, and yet I feel his wonderful eyes upon me and his soft, cool cheek against mine. . . . Once when we spoke about sex, Daddy told me that I couldn't

possibly understand belonging yet; I always knew that I did understand it, and now I understand it fully.[1]

Have you ever felt that way?

Your Desire for Popularity

As your sex becomes an increasingly important part of who you are, the pressures within you increase to gain popularity and acceptance. It has always meant a great deal to be accepted, even when you were younger. You wanted attention:

Look at me ride my bike.
Look at me jump.
Look at me run.
Look at me swim.

Now, however, acceptance means even more. The kind of attention you will want now is expressed like this:

Look at me, I have a boyfriend.
Look at me, I shave.
Look at me, I have a date this weekend.
Look at me, I was asked to a slumber party.
Look at me, I was elected an officer.

Your Temptations

When you are concerned with popularity and what people think of you, you are also tempted to use your power (which includes your sex) to manipulate people rather than love them. Erich Fromm put it like this: "We were created to love people and use things, but we have loved things and used people."

Have you ever asked such questions as these

---

[1] *Anne Frank: The Diary of a Young Girl*, Modern Library, New York, 1952, p. 148.

—How can I get that boy to like me?

—How can I work it so that I will be invited to that party?

—How will I have to change to be accepted by that group?

We can use our sexuality for getting people to do what we want them to do. It's a temptation we never outgrow. The problem, however, is one that is heightened for teenagers.

Some Guidelines

Now what does all of this have to do with joining the People of God and as a true follower of Jesus Christ walking in newness of life? Plenty! If we believe that Christ is Lord and that he has made all things new, we are given a new perspective on all of life, including sex and knowing who we are as sexual beings. Let's try to put down some guidelines that may encourage you to do some thinking on your own about your sexuality and the decisions it will require of you.

Sex is Good

We have talked about your changing bodies, your new feelings, which are sometimes mixed up, your desire to be popular, some of the temptations you are bound to meet. Actually, this is only another way of saying that this is the way God has created you. It means that your sexuality is good. In fact, it is one of the very best things about you, for it can enrich the life of another person as well as your own. This means

—*for girls only:*
Your femaleness is something with which you were born. God has endowed you with the marvelous potentialities for becoming a woman. Be glad for the traits and characteristics that make you different from boys.

Develop these gifts so that you will be prepared to play your proper role in the home and in society.

—*for boys only:*
Your maleness is God's gift to you. There is something great about being a male. But it's not something you need to prove. You can be what you are. Now is the time to begin developing your maleness for playing your essential role in society as provider, as worker and community-builder, and as a warm, human being capable of deep, caring relationships with other people.

—*for boys and girls:*
Your differences are given to you by God to complete what is lacking in the other. Together in your differing physical and psychological make-ups you are called to serve God as his partners in the world.

Now, let's look again at the two stories of creation in Genesis 1:27–31 and 2:18–25 and check out the following:

(1) God presents his image as two different kinds: male and female. Each is special. (2) Although they are different, each finds the fulness of his being in relation to the other. A literal translation of the Hebrew in Genesis 2:23 expresses Adam's joy in seeing woman for the first time: "This is the moment! Bone of my bones and flesh of my flesh!
(3) Both male and female have special tasks to do.
(4) God saw that everything he made, including sex, was good. This means that we are to be thankful that God has made us sexual creatures.

It is further interesting to note that when the Old Testament talks about the sexual act, it uses the expression "to know." "Now Adam knew Eve his wife" (Genesis 4:1). That means that the sexuality with which God has created male and female is not only the means by which the human race is perpetuated but is also the means of deepest fellowship and sharing by husband and wife in the marriage relationship.

Control is Vital

When you were delivered into the world, one of the strongest drives you were given was your sex. But like every other power, the sex drive must be controlled or it runs wild and becomes destructive. For example, electricity is a great natural force. Under control, it can

—cook your food
—keep your house warm in winter
—cool it in summer
—entertain you with radio or TV
—keep the world running smoothly

But running wild, as lightning, it can destroy in a few minutes what has taken years to build.

So it is with the sexual drive. If it is not controlled, it can hurt and destroy others and leave deep scars on you. If brought under control, it can become the basis of the finest friendships, the deepest love, and the happiest marriage and home that you can imagine. How you manage the drive and use it is crucial. Your church believes that your sex drive must always be the servant of love, of family, and of home.

Respect for Persons

Finally, the key to handling this wonderful gift of God is respect. Just as we want to be treated with respect, so we must show respect in all our relationships with others. God has placed us here to live for others as Christ did. That's what gives the Christian life its style.

Dr. Martin Buber, the Jewish philosopher, had a very important insight on which he built his philosophy. He said that man has two kinds of relationships:

"I-It" and "I-Thou"

Each involves a different kind of knowing and responding.

> I-It means that one looks at the other person as a thing, something to be used for one's own ends, or even as an object to be consumed as you would a candy bar or coke.
>
> I-Thou means that one looks at the other as a person in his own right, a person with integrity, gifts, and a personality to be cherished.

The moment you treat another person as a thing he becomes an "It" rather than a person in his own right, a beloved child of God. Each of us knows deep inside himself that the only kind of life that will ever make sense is one in which the I-Thou relationship is primary. This is the kind of love of which Paul speaks:

> "Love is patient and kind; it is not arrogant or rude. . . . does not insist on its own way; it is not irritable or resentful; it does not rejoice at wrong, but rejoices in the right. Love bears all things, believes all things, hopes all things, endures all things. . . . So faith, hope, love abide, these three; but the greatest of these is love."
>
> (1 Corinthians 13:4–7,13)

As you seek to help others grow in their appreciation of one another, one day when you establish a home of your own the questions we have been struggling with all our lives, like the question "Who am I?" will shift a little, and as husband and wife you will ask: "Who are we?" and "How can we live for others and so serve God and his world?"

Prayer

Father in heaven, be my close companion always. Protect me from costly mistakes that would mar me for life. Let me lean heavily upon you, for you are my strength in every temptation. Help me always to be courageous in standing for the right. Aid me in keeping the flame of love for all people burning brightly in my life that the radiance of love may be reflected into the lives of others. May I joyfully and happily serve you. May my faith be not merely one of habit but one of commitment to the higher, nobler way of life in you. I ask this in Jesus' name. Amen.

Some Things To Do

1. In magazines such as *Life* and *Look* find advertisements that attempt to sell products by using sex. You may wish to write up TV commercials instead. Bring these samples to class. Describe what such advertisements express about sex and about the worth of persons. Instead of this you may wish to find pictures that symbolize for you the American male or female.

2. In one or two paragraphs interpret what one of the following statements is attempting to say about love:

   a. "Being in love is not a matter of standing and looking forever into one another's eyes, but of turning and looking together at the world." (Source unknown)

   b. "Love is the only way to grasp another human being in the innermost core of his personality. No one can become fully aware of the very essence of another human being unless he loves him. By the spiritual act of love he is enabled to see the essential traits and features in the beloved person; and even more, he sees that which is potential in him, that which is not yet actualized but yet ought to be actualized. Furthermore, by his love, the loving person enables the beloved person to actualize these potentialities. By making him aware of what he can be and of what he should become, he makes these potentialities come true." [2]

---

[2] Viktor Frankl, *Man's Search for Meaning,* (Washington Square Press, 1963), p. 176–177.

c. "Adherence to Jesus allows us no free rein to desire unless it is accompanied by love." (Dietrich Bonhoeffer)

3. Read Ephesians 5:21–33

a. Read the passage aloud and then silently.

b. Restate in your own words what Paul has said.

c. What do you think Paul means when he says that Christ's act of dying on the cross is like marriage?

d. Are there any guidelines in these instructions that might apply to dating?

4. Compose a prayer or a poem that celebrates your sexuality.

5. Be prepared to discuss the following:

a. What basis is there for saying that jokes about sex are a form of profanity?

b. Do you think the use of sex to sell products is a cause or an effect of our society's being saturated with sex?

c. There are times when people think they are drawing closer to one another when they are only using one another for their own selfish desires.

MEMORY WORK

What is sanctification?

Sanctification is that work of the Holy Spirit by which he cleanses us from sin and enables us to live a new life according to Christ's example.

"Let not sin therefore reign in your mortal bodies, to make you obey their passions. Do not yield your members to sin as instruments of wickedness, but yield yourselves to God as men who have been brought from death to life, and your members to God as instruments of righteousness" (*Romans 6:12, 13*).

Glorious Things of Thee Are Spoken

Glorious things of thee are spoken, Zion, city of our God;
He, whose word cannot be broken, Formed thee for His own
  abode;
On the Rock of Ages founded, What can shake thy sure
  repose?
With salvation's walls surrounded, Thou may'st smile at all
  thy foes.

See, the streams of living waters, Springing from eternal
  love,
Well supply thy sons and daughters, And all fear of want
  remove:
Who can faint, while such a river Ever flows their thirst
  t'assuage?
Grace which, like the Lord, the Giver, Never fails from age
  to age.

Round each habitation hov'ring, See the cloud and fire ap-
  pear
For a glory and a cov'ring, Showing that the Lord is near!
Glorious things of thee are spoken, Zion, city of our God;
He, whose word cannot be broken, Formed thee for His own
  abode.

—The Hymnal

Unit 6
Signs
of New Life

Photo by Thomas Medcalf

19

Baptized into the World

The Mystery of the Waters

IN THE PLAY "The Miracle Worker" the climax comes when Helen Keller, deprived of sight, hearing, and speech suddenly understands the meaning of a word. It happens like this. Her teacher, Annie Sullivan, is pumping water from the well. As the water pours over one of Helen's hands, the teacher taps out the word in the other, w-a-t-e-r. First slowly, then quickly, until the light dawns. For the first time in her life Helen catches the relationship between the word and the thing. And the world opens up to her. All of the pent-up frustration and loneliness, all of the hunger to know and to relate to others, is suddenly released. Now everything has a name. You almost feel it happening to you as you watch the blind girl lurching from object to object, begging that the name be written on her hand by the teacher.

The Power of the Word

In this breakthrough into a new world by a single word, Helen Keller came to life as a person. The word built a bridge between teacher and girl and between girl and world. By the power of the word, she was restored to the world from which she had been isolated. It happened because of word plus water plus teacher. The whole action together was the miracle.

Means of Grace

In a similar way, God sets up his communications system with us. He does this by certain signs through which he draws near to speak his word in order to restore and renew us. We call these signs "means of grace."

If you had been able to visit the Temple in Jerusalem in the days of the ancient People of God, you would have noticed these signs

—the veil that covered the Holy of Holies
—the showbread placed in front of the veil
—water jars for the rites of purification, etc.

These were some of the signs and symbols through which the ancient People of God encountered Yahweh. They were reminders of his presence, his power and goodness, by means of which they experienced a deeper love for him. Through such sacred signs they were also helped to renew their faith and loyalty to Yahweh.

As you enter your own church, you will notice many sacred signs, things like

—pictures
—symbols
—a cross
—candlesticks

As the congregation gathers for worship, you will notice signs which are more dramatic like

—reading and preaching from a book
—praying
—washing with water
—eating and drinking

We call these signs which require action "means of grace," a communications system by which God tells us what he is like and how much he desires to have fellowship with us. The means of grace which seem most important and helpful to the People of God are

—the Word, that is, the Bible both as written and proclaimed
—prayer
—the Sacraments

That is why you are asked this question when you join the church:

"Do you promise in watchfulness and prayer to diligently use the Word of God and the Holy Sacraments?"

But now we have a problem:

> Sacraments are means of grace, but not all means of grace are sacraments. And so we must ask: What is a sacrament?

Among the early Christians baptism and the Lord's Supper were regarded as special—in a sense, secret—acts of worship. In Greek they were sometimes called *mysterion* (pronounced miss-tare-e-on). You can almost figure out the meaning for yourself. Baptism and the Lord's Supper were mysteries which dramatized the great mystery of God's redeeming love.

Later, the Greek word *mysterion* was translated into the Latin word *sacramentum,* from which we get our English word "sacrament." The Latin word referred to an oath of allegiance given by a soldier to his commander. What had been something secret was now something public.

In a definition that has become classic and which we offer to you as a working-definition, Augustine said that

> "A sacrament is the visible and outward sign of an invisible and spiritual grace."

Two Sacraments

Though Protestants are far from agreed as to the exact meaning of the sacraments, wc arc at least agreed that there are two: baptism and the Lord's Supper. The reason we have reached agreement on two sacraments (Roman Catholics have seven) is that

1. we have the clear word of Jesus himself commanding that these two acts be done;
2. these two acts clearly proclaim the gospel message— the Good News of God's love for men.

We might also add that Protestants are agreed that there is nothing magical about them. Faith is essential to receiving the sacraments.

Just as everything became new for Helen Keller through the action of word plus water plus teacher, so it is for those who in watchfulness and prayer diligently use the Word of God and the holy sacraments. If there is a formula, it might sound like this:

> Word (the message of God's love) plus material things like water or bread and wine plus people who care—these proclaim God's love, enable us to ponder his offer of new life and to show forth our true allegiance in service to the world.

The Sacrament of Baptism

Notice how many different images of baptism are to be found in the New Testament:

> Death and resurrection—Romans 6:3, Col. 2:12, 3:1–4
> Putting on Christ—Galatians 3:26–29; Col. 3:9ff.
> Washing—Titus 3:5–8; 1 Cor. 6:11, Eph. 5:25
> Seal of the Spirit—2 Cor. 1:21, 22; Eph. 1:13, 14; 4:30
> Circumcision—Col. 2:11, 12
> Deliverance from bondage—1 Cor. 10:1, 2; 1 Peter 3:18–21
> New Birth—John 3:3–8

It soon becomes clear that you can't wrap up all that the New Testament says about baptism in a neat package. However, you can begin to sense the importance baptism had for the early Christians and why it was the sacrament of entrance into the church.

In *A Book of Worship for Covenant Churches* baptism is summarized as ". . . a sign and seal of our cleansing, of our engrafting into Christ, and of our welcome into the household of God." [1]

---

[1] *A Book of Worship for Covenant Churches*, (Chicago, Covenant Press, 1964), p. 57.

You will also discover in most constitutions for Covenant churches statements like this:

> "Only such persons as by confession of faith and Christian living attest that they are true believers in the Lord Jesus Christ and who are baptized in the name of the Father, the Son, and the Holy Spirit shall be admitted to membership in this church."

So baptism has many rich meanings. And baptism is essential to joining the People of God.

You Are Special

But now let me try to relate this sacrament to your life so that you feel the cool stream gushing over one hand while I spell out the word in the other. First of all, baptism says that you are special.

You have heard that before. That's what the Good News says about you. But baptism is the visible sign that it is so. When you are baptized, your name is spoken as if to say:

> For you, ____, Christ came, entered the waters of the Jordan, went into the wilderness of temptation, healed, taught, and finally, at a place called Calvary, drank the cup alone, went down into the depths of misery and death, and bare-handed fought the battle, mastered the enemies of your sin and death, and won. This Man died for you. This Man was raised up for you. You are loved, accepted, forgiven.

Whenever you see someone baptized, it should be a reminder to you of your own baptism. It is the Good News made visible, proclaiming how special you are to God and to the church and what you are called to be as this special person.

We sometimes forget that we are someone special to God. Perhaps right now you feel there is no one in the world as worthless as you. You've tried being a Christian, but you've failed. You would worship God in a minute if only you could feel that somehow he was near you, helping you, caring about you. Remember that there is comfort for you.

When things were rough and he needed encouragement in his faith, Martin Luther would scrawl out the words "I was baptized"—as if to say: "Despite the way I feel, God loves me and always has. God loves me and always will. God has placed his mark on me, and once he has promised something, he will never go back on his word."

If you have not been baptized, it doesn't mean you are any less important to God. But baptism proclaims the truth that you are special. Actually, there is no better time to request baptism than when you are confirmed. Your pastor will welcome the opportunity to counsel with you further if you will indicate your desire.

You Have Relatives

Baptism is not only personal; it involves others. When you are baptized, you are surrounded by all kinds of people who care about you:

—father and mother
—brothers and sisters
—grandfathers and grandmothers
—uncles and aunts
—sponsors or godparents

You might be tempted to conclude that baptism really belongs in the home as a family affair. But this is not true. Baptism is an act that involves the whole family of God so that in addition to your flesh-and-blood relatives, there is a congregation that assumes responsibility for you and your future. That's why the service of baptism is celebrated in public worship. It involves the whole People of God.

But there are other relatives too, those you didn't choose but who are given to you in your baptism. St. Paul reminds us:

"For Christ is like a single body with its many limbs and organs, which, many as they are, together make up one body. For indeed we were all brought into one body by baptism, in the one Spirit, whether we are Jews or Greeks, whether slaves or free men, and that one Holy Spirit was poured out for all of us to drink."

(1 Corinthians 12:12,13, *New English Bible*)

Further, he says that baptism erases all distinctions that tend to make us different from each other, things like culture, class, and race:

"Baptized into union with him, you have all put on Christ as a garment. There is no such thing as Jew and Greek, slave and freeman, male and female; for you are all one person in Christ Jesus."

(Galatians 3:27,28, *New English Bible*)

You have many relatives, for in your baptism you become a brother of all other Christians. You are called to love and care for them even as they are called to love and care for you.

You Belong to Christ

In baptism, you become Christ's own possession. Not only is your name spoken, but his Name is spoken over you, thereby making you a marked person. From that moment on, you bear the mark of Jesus Christ. Speaking of the early church, one great scholar says:

"At baptism they [the early Christians] swore to him the military oath, they promised themselves to Christ, they now belong to him and as his soldiers are responsible to him only." [2]

Belonging to Christ, however, can be costly. It means you are linked together with his death and resurrection. As baptism signified the way of life through death for Jesus, those who bear his Name must follow the same way. You hear this theme coming through loud and clear in St. Paul.

---

[2] Hans-Ruedi Weber, *The Militant Ministry*, (Philadelphia, Fortress Press, 1963), p. 7. Quoted from Adolph Harnack.

Read Romans 6 again:

—baptized into Christ
—into his death
—buried with him
—united with him in a death like his
—united in a resurrection like his
—crucified with him
—died with him
—live with him

To put it as simply as I can: You die to your little gods, to your phoney values, to the self that wants its own comfort and ease, to your own homemade righteousness, to conformity to the world that is opposed to God in order to be free for service to the world, free to give yourself to others without fear of what's going to happen to you. You are raised up, which means you live under the promise that the Lord's servants do not love and suffer and die in vain. If you really belong to Christ in this costing way, it follows that you are sent forth into the world.

That was what Jesus' baptism meant to him. It was the way he came to know his task. It marked his consecration to be the Messiah. He said it was "to fulfill all righteousness," that is, to do what other men were called to do. The Spirit that came upon him at his baptism did not rescue him from the world but sent him forth renewed and empowered for his task in the world.

For Helen Keller, water and the word administered by a loving teacher marked her real entry into the world. The old frustration, loneliness, and fear were washed away in the flow of water, and everything had a name. So in your baptism. You are consecrated and jet-propelled into the world

—to be there for others
—to love and serve
—to break through all barriers which separate man from man

—to join in his struggle for the world
—to fight against its enemies
—to proclaim its rightful Lord

Thus, in our baptism we are both taken out of the world and sent back into the world as servants of Christ. You should be able to locate the People of God wherever service is required.

Infants or Adults?

Because baptism represents a life-long commitment to Jesus Christ and to the world he came to redeem, the questions of when and how should never be of major importance. Like the marriage ceremony, the act is over in a matter of minutes while the action and what it signifies takes a lifetime. More important than when and how is to know what is promised and given and to what one is being called. The formula remains the same for both forms of baptism: whenever word plus water plus caring people return us to the world in newness of life, then you discover the mystery of the waters.

Prayer

Don't let this be simply a social occasion, Jesus. Touch the hearts of those present who associate Christianity only with superficiality and have become accustomed to religious exercises devoid of integrity or real meaning. Someone is being baptized into your own life and death, Lord. . . . Don't let this baptism be shunted off into a small corner of a big church, or into a quiet hour with a handful of people. Let this baptism be a principal part of the whole church's life, Jesus. Make us all realize that we are profoundly involved in it because someone is being ordained to a lifetime of discipleship and ministry in your spirit and name. Amen.

—Malcolm Boyd [3]

---

[3] Malcolm Boyd, *Are You Running With Me Jesus?* (New York, Avon Books, 1967), p. 131.

Some Things To Do

1. Browse through the Gospels and list instances where Jesus used signs and gestures as he encountered people.

2. Make a list and explain the meaning of some of the signs we use in our daily life such as a frown, a scowl, a smile, a handshake, a salute to the flag, and so forth.

3. Draw and explain the symbols you find in your church building.

4. Read Romans 6, then make two lists of words:

   a. words that describe us without baptism

   b. words that describe us as truly baptized

   Try to translate these words into words and ideas that are meaningful to you.

5. In one of the old churches of Europe (the cathedral of Ghent) there is an unusual baptismal font. It is in the form of a giant globe taller than a man. Coiled around the globe is a serpent and on top is a cross. The globe is in halves. Above it is a large pulley and chain to lift the top half of the font when there is to be a baptism. Inside is the water. Beside the globe-like font is a candlestick with a huge candle that is lighted at the time of baptism. Write an essay on what you think the artist intended to say in designing this baptismal font.

6. Be prepared to discuss in class the following:

   a. On infant baptism: "A newborn child is the beginning of an immortal soul, but is not yet an independent soul. Decisions have to be made for him, by his parents and by the Church, and these cannot be postponed, because life goes on and the child grows up in one way or another. So the Christian Church and Christian parents will choose the Christian life for their children. Does this mean that the benefits of the sacrament come to the child in response to the faith of the parents and of the Church? Yes, indeed; that is just what it means. They claim God's promise for the child, by faith. And that is just as it ought to be, and is in keeping with the whole outlook of the New Testament . . ." [4]

b. On adult baptism: "Baptism is in the New Testament the indispensable answer to an unavoidable question made by the man who comes to faith. . . . In baptism a restoration is called for. What is demanded is very simple: in place of the present infant baptism a responsible baptism on the part of the person being baptized. He must, if things are to be done right, become once again not a passive object of baptism but the free partner of Jesus Christ, who decides for himself, confesses for himself, and testifies for himself to his own willingness and readiness." [5]

c. On the practice of Covenant churches: "Although the major practice of Covenant churches has always been, and still is, that of infant baptism, it has nevertheless been recognized that Christian people have, through the ages, interpreted the Scriptures differently with respect to baptism. Believing that membership in the church is determined solely on the basis of personal faith in Christ as Lord and Savior, it refuses to divide the church because of doctrinal differences which do not disturb the central verities of the faith. In accordance with its doctrine of freedom within the limits of the Scriptures and the living tradition of the church, the Covenant permits the practice of either infant or adult baptism. A corollary of this freedom, obviously, is the obligation of every Covenant minister to administer either of these recognized modes of baptism. It naturally follows that no Covenant minister is free to present his interpretation of baptism as if it were the only proper viewpoint and practice. In brief, he must be willing not only to accept Covenant freedom for himself but allow it to others." [6]

d. On baptism as integration: "To discriminate against others because they are not like us in superficial ways is to forget the testimony of baptism: Those who have been baptized are like us in all that matters. They have been accepted by God, and who are we to find them unacceptable to us? It is tragic that many Christians have failed to see

[4] Donald M. Baillie, *The Theology of the Sacraments*, (Scribners and Sons, 1957), pp. 82–83.
[5] Jack Finegan, *First Steps in Theology*, (Association Press, 1960), pp. 105–106.
[6] *A Book of Worship for Covenant Churches*, op. cit., pp. 233–234.

that baptism provides the strongest possible case for the acceptance of Christians whose skin may be of a different color. Refusal to accept the baptized is a form of blasphemy, a denial that God's activity in baptism has any reality at all." [7]

[7] James F. White, *The Worldliness of Worship*, (Oxford University Press, 1967), pp. 151–152.

MEMORY WORK

What is a sacrament?

A sacrament is a visible and outward sign of an invisible and spiritual grace. The sacraments commanded by Jesus Christ are baptism and the Lord's Supper.

"So those who received his word were baptized, and there were added that day about three thousand souls. And they devoted themselves to the apostles' teaching and fellowship, to the breaking of bread and the prayers" (*Acts 2:41, 42*).

What is baptism?

Baptism is the sacred use of water which was commanded by Jesus Christ to signify God's cleansing of our sins and our consecration to God.

"Go therefore and make disciples of all nations, baptizing them in the name of the Father and of the Son and of the Holy Spirit, teaching them to observe all that I have commanded you; and lo, I am with you always, to the close of the age" (*Matthew 28:19, 20*).

20

Here
We Offer

For My Recalling

Sunday	*1 Corinthians 11:23–26* Do This . . .
Monday	*Mark 14:22–25* A New Agreement
Tuesday	*John 6:52–59* Bread of Life
Wednesday	*John 15:1–11* True Vine
Thursday	*1 Corinthians 10:14–17* One Loaf, One Body
Friday	*Matthew 5:21–24* A Peace Offering
Saturday	*Philippians 2:14–18* A Costly Offering

CAN YOU RECALL how you first experienced love? Probably not, for you can't remember that far back. When you were a baby and woke up, you were hungry. Actually, you felt hunger as real pain. You bawled your lungs out crying for food. The simple act of giving food relieved the pain. As a result you got the message even though you couldn't understand it: "We love you."

Each time you woke up because of that pain in your stomach you became more and more aware of the important people in your life, your mother, especially. Those people were important because they met your needs, particularly your need for food. As they gave you food, you learned how they felt about you. That experience of becoming aware of other people has been a part of your becoming you.

Food and Love

Of course, food is more than a way of getting rid of the pain in your stomach. The most ordinary meal stands for right relationships or the lack of them. If you have had a fight with your brother or sister just before supper, you know how miserable your food tastes. If eating were just a matter of potatoes and gravy, then you would enjoy eating no matter how you felt about that brother or sister.

If food is to taste right and be digested properly, it must be truly shared, thus symbolizing our oneness with each other. If it is truly shared, mealtime becomes the most important time of the day. This is often true of the evening meal, when you are together as a family. Then you have time to reflect on what has happened during the day—who said what, and how unfair that teacher grades, who is having the next slumber party, and so forth. If your eating together is an act of real sharing, you will discover as you grow older that much of the meaning of family life is centered around the dinner table.

Food and Others

Food is also a great socializer, from the first date to the senior prom right up to the receiving ambassadors from foreign countries. Whether it's a coke and fries or a formal dinner, eating together is the most common social act of our lives. Sitting down with someone else at the same table and talking together can shape and change attitudes. A famous educator and psychologist, Dr. Bruno Bettelheim, sees food as a means of therapy. He gives these illustrations:

Case One: For deprived children, it has been proven that when small groups of such children eat together with their teachers, they begin to feel themselves a part of the group and so begin to learn.

Case Two: In mental hospitals, levels of tension are instantly lowered and positive attitudes emerge when patients, doctors, and staff all eat the same kind of food and eat it together.

The Lord's Supper

It's not strange then that the most important single act of our worship as the People of God should be sharing in a meal. Despite the importance we tend to attach to so-called spiritual acts like

—singing hymns
—praying
—reading the Bible
—thinking
—believing

we need to let the plain, blunt comment of C. S. Lewis sink in:

There's no good trying to be more spiritual than God. God never meant man to be a purely spiritual creature. That's why he uses material things like bread and wine to put new life into us. We may think this rather crude and unspiritual. God doesn't. He invented eating. He likes matter. He invented it.[1]

So God communicates his love and forgiveness to us. By sharing a common meal, we are able

1) to see and marvel at a love too deep for words
2) to act out physically our need for love
3) to receive love as a gift

We don't have to understand it all, any more than we have to understand biochemistry in order to eat our meals and be nourished. All we need to do is to take the food God offers.

The Last Supper

But how did this family meal of God's People begin? It probably had its origin in the most important meal of the ancient People of God, the Passover. Jesus wanted to eat this meal with his disciples as a reminder of the mighty acts of God for his people.

Then, of course, it was the last meal Jesus was to eat with his disciples. All of them never ate together again, at least, not in the same way as that night in the upper room. In many respects, it was probably like many other occasions when they had eaten together, except for the terror that clutched at their hearts. The disciples had good reason to know it might be the last time together.

As Jesus spoke to them, he did something he had never done before. Taking up a loaf of bread and breaking it in his hands, he said: "This is my body which is broken for you." It was as if he were saying, I die willingly for your sake just as I now break the bread for your sake. Then later, he took the cup of wine, which he said was "the new

---

[1] C. S. Lewis, *The Case for Christianity* (New York, Macmillan Company, 1951), p. 55.

covenant in my blood." In giving them the bread and the cup, he was not thinking of the pain in their stomachs but was inviting them to share his life, to take his life into themselves, to live out both the suffering and the joy of it. For all the centuries since then, the church has been re-enacting this last supper in obedience to his command: "Do this in remembrance of me." By actually doing it, we are given a visible, tangible sign

- —of his offering, the giving away of his life for the sake of the world
- —of our sharing in this life, giving ourselves away for the sake of the world

The Service

Now let's take this action in slow motion. Imagine you are in church. It's Sunday morning again. The Lord's Supper is being celebrated. Whatever else happens in the service, you can predict that the most ancient account of the institution of the Supper will be read. You can check it out for yourself in 1 Corinthians 11:23–26. Then with that clear directive before the congregation, your pastor will literally repeat or act out the four things Jesus did at the last meal he had with his disciples.

1. Jesus "took bread" just as after the meal he took the cup. So your pastor "takes" the elements of bread and wine and prepares them for the holy use to which they are appointed.

2. Jesus "gave thanks." So your pastor consecrates the elements, that is, offers them up to God for his blessing, and gives thanks. That best expresses the true spirit of the meal. It is not a funeral but a joyous feast.

3. Jesus "broke it," just as later he poured out the wine. So your pastor breaks a piece of bread and pours out wine as reminders that bread cannot be shared unless

first broken, even as Christ's life could not be fully shared until it was broken in death.

4. Jesus "gave" the bread and the wine. So your pastor gives the bread and the wine to the deacons, who distribute the meal—not simply as bread and wine but as his body broken for them and his blood shed for them. This represents his real presence with them.

The Meaning of the Meal

However simple the action of the Last Supper, the meaning of this sacrament is rich and diverse. This is indicated by the several names given to the meal. Each name indicates a special meaning of the sacrament:

Eucharist, one of the earliest names given to the meal and becoming more common among Christians today, is derived from the Greek word eucharistia (pronounced you-cah-wrist-ee-ah). It means thanksgiving. Though it is not used in the New Testament in reference to the Lord's Supper, the usage developed soon after the New Testament was written. It reflects the words of institution: "He gave thanks," thereby pointing to the chief characteristic of the service: the People of God saying thank-you for Christ, his life and death and resurrection, and his undying love.

Mass is the name most commonly used by Roman Catholics. Though this term is not found in the New Testament, it points to the costly sacrifice which God has made on man's behalf and which Catholics believe is repeated when the priest offers up to God the bread and the wine.

Lord's Supper is perhaps the name most frequently used by Protestants. This term stresses the fact that it is the meal which re-enacts "the night in which he was betrayed" and which therefore continues the table fellowship of Jesus with his disciples.

Sacrament of the Altar is a term used most often by Lutherans. It points to the place of offering where Christ was sacrificed once for all and where believers become one with his sacrifice.

Holy Communion is another term Christians commonly use when speaking of this sacrament. It stresses three facets of the meal:

—fellowship with the crucified and risen Lord
—union with all fellow believers
—identification with those in Christ who have preceded us in death.

In *A Book of Worship for Covenant Churches,* the Service of Holy Communion indicates the difficulty we have of telling all that this sacrament means to us. Notice the diversity of meanings in the reminder given to the congregation:

> Fellow believers, as we come to the Lord's Table, we are to remember with gratitude that our Lord instituted this Sacrament as a communion of his body and blood, given and shed for the remission of sins; for the memory of his dying for our sakes and the assurance of his undying love; as a bond of our union with him and with each other as members of his body, the church; as a seal of his promises to us and a renewal of our obedience to him; for the blessed assurance of his presence with us who are gathered here in his name; and as a pledge of his coming again.[2]

We have spoken a great deal of God's action in this sacrament—what he gives and promises. God has offered up his only Son. Jesus has offered up his life. This meal is his gift to us. By it we are forgiven and fed. We know ourselves loved and accepted as his people. For this we are grateful.

But is there nothing we can offer?

You have probably noticed in the Sunday morning bulletin an item called "The Offertory." It is that point in the

---

[2] *A Book of Worship for Covenant Churches, op. cit.,* p. 73.

service when the organist plays something special or the choir sings an anthem while the ushers receive the offering. It's probably the time when you look up at the ceiling or daydream or get fidgety, but in the early church it was one of the most dramatic moments of the service. It was the time when the whole congregation could get into the act. At that point certain members would come forward with gifts of money and other presents for the poor and also the gifts of bread and wine for the communion meal

—bread baked in some Christian housewife's kitchen
—wine from some Christian's vineyard.

These everyday gifts, together with money, represented daily work. These things were offered to God to become "means of grace," returning things and persons to what they were meant to be and therefore consecrating all of life to God. Preaching to the newly-confirmed at Easter, Augustine said: "There you are upon the Table: there you are in the Chalice (the Cup)."

Your Offering

What can you offer? Here are some of the things you can bring:

—your time (approximately 15,000 hours of TV in 15 years)
—your money
—your brains and talents
—your words
—your friendship and love

You offer what is yours, not what belongs to someone else. You can't say: "If only I had his brains, then . . ."; or, "If only I had her money, then . . . ." No, you offer what you are now. You offer whatever you have, the things you are most proud of and most secure in doing, the things you do best.

To "rightly use the sacraments," which is what you promise when you join the People of God, means not only that you have something to receive but that you have something to give. While he wants what you can offer, he wants you most of all. And this includes some other things:

—what you like least
—what you do the poorest
—where you feel you are the greatest failure

He wants you to offer yourself just the way you are. For that's how he loves you and how he can best use you as a sign of Christ's body in the world.

> "Consecrate us, body and soul, to be a living, acceptable offering unto thee, so that in word and deed we may continually praise and glorify thy holy name."

Prayer

> Jesus, we're here again. What are we doing here? I mean, how is communion with you possible? You're holy, and we're very human. Yet I remember that you also became human.
>
> I wonder how we can honestly be nourished and cleansed by your body and blood. Yet I realize communion is an outward and visible sign of an inward and spiritual grace. I accept this mystery.
>
> We are grateful for this intimacy with you, Jesus. We thank you for letting us share this corporate action as we offer to God all of creation including our own lives. Give us faith to understand what it means to be thankful. Amen.
>
> —Malcolm Boyd [3]

---

[3] Boyd, *op. cit.*, p. 130.

Some Things To Do

1. Read 1 Corinthians 11:18–34 and answer the following questions:

   a. What was Paul unhappy about?

   b. What do you think he means by "discerning the body"?

   c. What does he mean by eating and drinking unworthily?

   d. Why can't you eat and drink the Lord's Supper without regard for your fellow believers?

   e. How would you relate what Paul says to life today?

2. Tell in a brief essay how you think a person should prepare to receive the Lord's Supper. Do you consider confirmation as a part of this preparation?

3. Study the observance of the Lord's Supper and its meaning in the following churches in your community:

   > Roman Catholic
   > Greek Orthodox
   > Lutheran
   > Episcopal
   > Methodist
   > Baptist

   Your pastor may wish to assign members of the class to interview the ministers or priests of these churches, or he may indicate reference books where you can get the information.

4. Complete the following story: The night before communion was to be celebrated a group of senior-highs asked the pastor if they could bring a new kind of offering—not envelopes containing money but a bit of their life, work and play, the things that meant most to them in their daily lives. That morning they came to worship with footballs, books, report cards, personal letters, and teddy bears. They covered the communion table with their offerings. Then each one told why he had brought a particular offering. It was not like sealed envelopes or secret pledges. It was all laid open there before the people and the Lord. When the bread and wine were consecrated, so were the things they brought. It was the consecration of their lives. When the service was

over, they left and took their offerings with them. Some said that the things that meant most to them seemed new. None of it had been on an altar before. They had come to see that all their work and life was on an altar. If I had been present, I would have brought _____.
What difference do you think it would make to have something that means a great deal to you consecrated to the Lord?

5. Be prepared to discuss the following in class:

a. How do we continue the action of Holy Communion in everyday life? at the dinner table? at the lunchroom table at school? at a meeting table?

b. How do bread and wine as used in the Lord's Supper suggest our dependence on the world?

c. Do you think it would be difficult for a person whose family table has been a place of quarreling to find meaning in coming to the Lord's Table?

d. How could the celebration of the Lord's Supper in your congregation become more meaningful?

e. What is the significance of the way the Lord's Supper is distributed? For instance, in some churches the people go forward and kneel at an altar rail while in other churches the people are served in the pews.

f. Do you think the following experience represents the act of Holy Communion?

"I remember a Sunday morning in 1964, during a trip to Mississippi to assist in Negro voter registration. At the 'Freedom House' where I lived, I became deeply involved in a conversation with one of the student volunteers. She had not talked with an older person for quite some time about the things that mattered most to her, the pressing personal questions about life. She had so much to say that by the time we finished it was too late for me to attend morning worship. It had remained in my mind that it was Sunday morning, and I had planned to attend a worship service, although I knew it must be a Negro service or a white one. As always, I hated this particular sinful prospect. But then, suddenly, God's grace seemed simply and beautifully manifest to me. The student and I had broken toast and eaten it, had shared the coffee. Surely God had, in his providence and merciful love, permitted us to share in communion with him." [4]

[4] Malcolm Boyd, *Are You Running With Me Jesus, op. cit.,* p. 15.

MEMORY WORK

What is the Lord's Supper?

The Lord's Supper is the sacred use of bread and the cup which was commanded by Jesus Christ, by which we remember his suffering for us, proclaim his death until he comes, and in communion with one another partake of him in faith.

"For I received from the Lord what I also delivered to you, that the Lord Jesus on the night when he was betrayed took bread, and when he had given thanks, he broke it, and said, 'This is my body which is broken for you. Do this in remembrance of me.' In the same way also the cup after supper, saying, 'This cup is the new covenant in my blood. Do this, as often as you drink it, in remembrance of me.' For as often as you eat this bread and drink the cup, you proclaim the Lord's death until he comes" (*1 Corinthians 11:23–26*).

Lead On, O King Eternal

Lead on, O King Eternal, The day of march has come;
Henceforth in fields of conquest Thy tents shall be our
   home.
Thro' days of preparation Thy grace has made us strong,
And now, O King Eternal, We lift our battle song.

Lead on, O King Eternal, Till sin's fierce war shall cease,
And holiness shall whisper The sweet Amen of peace;
For not with swords loud clashing, Nor roll of stirring
   drums;
With deeds of love and mercy, The heav'nly kingdom
   comes.

Lead on, O King Eternal, We follow, not with fears;
For gladness breaks like morning Where'er Thy face ap-
   pears;
Thy cross is lifted o'er us; We journey in its light:
The crown awaits the conquest; Lead on, O God of might.
   Amen.

—The Hymnal

Unit 7
Joining in the Faith

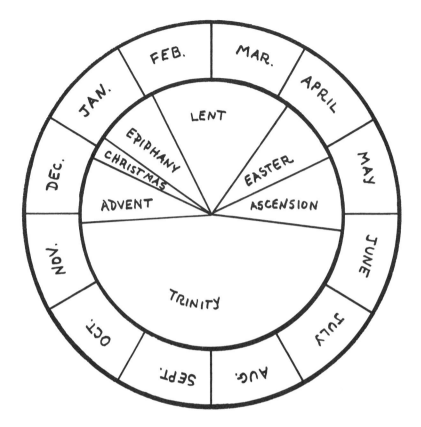

Fixed Dates:
New Year, Jan. 1
Epiphany, Jan. 6
Reformation Day, Oct. 31
All Saints Day, Nov. 1
Christmas, Dec. 25

Movable Dates:
Ash Wednesday, Feb. 4—Mar. 5
Palm Sunday, Mar. 15—April 18
Good Friday, Mar. 20—April 23
Easter Sunday, Mar. 22—April 25
Ascension Day, April 30—June 3
Pentecost, May 10—June 13
Trinity Sunday, May 17—June 20
First Sunday in Advent, Nov. 27—Dec. 3

21

Let Us Worship God

A People Gathered

FOLLOWING A SERVICE of worship where the Lord's Supper had been celebrated, Karen, who had been confirmed just a few months before and then received into the membership of the church, came to her pastor wearing a smile that made her whole face shine. "Pastor," she said, "I want you to know that *today* I joined the church!"

What do you think she meant? The service had been like all the others she had attended. What made this one different? Perhaps it was a hymn, or a prayer, or something the pastor said, or sharing in the bread and cup. Most likely it was all of these acts together, plus the Holy Spirit, that made worship come alive that morning. At any rate, Karen felt that now she belonged to the People of God. Now she knew who she was.

Worship as Something Natural

For many teenagers, worship is anything but enjoyable. More often than not, it's a bore! If you really get a kick out of it, there must be something wrong with you. Actually, it's the other way around. Worship is a natural part of our lives. We were made this way.

But let's check it out. The word worship (literally, "worthship," as you may recall) means to value or give worth to something or somebody or to bow down in submission.

> Whenever we give worth or value to the wrong thing or person, we become idolaters. Despite what we say we believe, what we attach the most value to is really our god.

> Whenever we give worth to the true and living God, we are saying how much he is worth and how much we want to be his People.

In either case, however, we are worshipping. We are doing what comes naturally!

Worship and Life

You may recall that we used a Greek word *leitourgia* (literally, "the people's work") to describe the worship of the early church. We made the point that the people's work or liturgy referred originally to all that the People of God did as a result of their new life in Christ. Only later did *leitourgia* come to be divided into two separate activities, with stress on special rites and ceremonies performed inside a church building.

As we dig into this matter of worship again and think about what goes on inside the church building, I want you to keep in mind the original meaning of *leitourgia* as "the people's work." Worship begins in the church building, but if it is the real thing, it must continue in the world outside. If you can tell where worship stops and work in the world begins or where work in the world stops and worship begins, then something is radically wrong. Worship in a church building and work in the world are both ways of acting out our relationship with God and other people. It is a way of demonstrating that the church is his and that the world is his.

Public Worship

This discovery that worship embraces all of life and enters into whatever we affirm and do is liberating, so liberating, in fact, that you may be tempted to ask, as many do: "If the world is God's sanctuary, and I can worship him every place, in every act, then why do I need to gather on Sunday morning for worship in a particular sanctuary?"

A good question! Most Christians would agree that we gather to worship because there is something different and special about worshipping together in one place. Here are a few reasons why:

—the need to express certain things together
—the need to reaffirm who we are

—the need to hear it like it is
—the need to be tested by the discipline of the group
—the need to be corrected and inspired by the Good News
—the need to receive our rations to live "out there"
—the need to be sent out to tell what we have seen and heard
—the need to be reminded in one place that God is in all places

In a sense, we come together to worship because we have to—not "have to" because our parents say so or the pastor says so or some other authority says so but because we are confronted by so many signs of God's love and care:

—the world he created
—the things we enjoy
—the people who care
—the forgiveness he offers

And so we worship gladly, saying

—Yes to life!
—Yes to the world!
—Yes to ourselves!
—Yes to God!

That's why the church asks you in the final question: "Do you promise to join us in worship . . . ?"

Joyous Celebration

Much of the resistance to worship on the part of teen-agers comes because it is routine and far from where they live. Have you ever felt like this:

What's wrong with the people in church?
What's the matter with them, Lord?
What happens to people
when they get inside a church?

Why do they change
and freeze up
when they get inside a church?
They don't seem to enjoy themselves
or talk to anyone.

They freeze up tight.
I know
because I've been watching them.

They look like penguins
standing on the shore
and staring at the weary ocean.

I watch them mumble through a melody
they've sung a thousand times or more
the way their tired parents sang it
for fifty years before. . . .[1]

But then maybe that's not worship at all. Just ceremonies. When you turn to the Bible, you get an altogether different feeling. There were those, I'm sure, for whom worship was anything but a joy. Yet when the ancient People of God heard the awe-inspiring blast of the ram's horn, or when the early Christians gathered in the upper room to wait for the Spirit, for most of them it was no static ceremony where everyone froze up tight. It was more like thirsty travellers lost in the desert suddenly coming on water, or like starved men finding bread. For Israel and for the disciples, their daily work offered to God created a need for worship. They were hungry for it. They knew their job was more than they could handle alone. They needed a word from God and the support of fellow believers to find strength for staying with the work to which God was calling them.

So coming together was something special. Everybody got into the act with everything he had. That's the kind of worship you find in the Psalms of the Old Testament. Listen to these expressions:

---

[1] Norman C. Habler, *For Mature Adults Only,* (Fortress Press, 1969).

"Sing a new song."
"Make a joyful noise to the Lord."
"Clap your hands, all peoples!"
"Shout to God with loud songs of joy!"
"Serve the Lord with gladness."
"Be glad and let the earth rejoice!"
"Let everything that breathes praise the Lord."

No "penguins" there! Those people weren't sitting on the side-lines letting the minister do it, mumbling their prayers, or going limp and numb and falling asleep. They were tremendously alive. Their bodies and minds were caught up in the act of celebrating:

clapping
shouting
dancing
marching
blowing horns
twanging stringed instruments

Of course, celebration is not joy only. It is also contrition, despair, pouring ashes on your head, pounding the ground and asking Why. But worship is primarily joy because the Word is, God is, we are.

This description of biblical worship needs, however, to bc brought down to where we can do some concrete thinking about what worship is or should be like.

Worship is Recital and Celebration

The word "recital" always sends shivers down my spine because it recalls those yearly ordeals at which I had to perform for a captive audience of beaming mothers and reluctant fathers by playing in the piano recital. After it was over, I felt like a prisoner who has just been pardoned. But recital as part of celebration is something good. It tells why we celebrate in the first place. We gather to rehearse

God's mighty acts in creation and history, particularly in the calling of his ancient people Israel and in his mightiest act of all, the giving of his Son Jesus Christ for man's salvation.

In the practice of many churches the clue for worship as celebration is provided by what is called the observance of the Christian Year. Such a calendar permits the festivity of worship to move from event to event, from remembrance to remembrance, in a way which tells the story of God's mighty acts in slow motion. Many pastors use what is called a *lectionary*, which is a list of Scripture lessons assigned for each Sunday of the year. There are four lessons that might be used on a given Sunday:

> *A Psalm*—permitting us to join our praises with the praises of Israel
> *An Old Testament lesson*—pointing us either to creation or to God's choice of Israel and the preparation of that people for the Messiah
> *A Gospel lesson*—witnessing to the Good News that God's promises have come true in Jesus
> *An Epistle lesson*—explaining and applying the Good News to the life of God's People in the church and the world

The Christian Year is divided into two parts:

1. The first half runs from Advent (which begins the Sunday nearest November 30) through Pentecost. It includes Advent, Christmas, Epiphany, Lent, Easter, Ascension, and Pentecost and stresses the events in the story of Christ.
2. The second half begins with Trinity Sunday and ends with Judgment Sunday. It stresses the response of the People of God to what God has done in Christ by a sacrificial style of life geared for action.

So whether singing, reading the Bible, preaching, reciting the Creed, baptizing, eating and drinking, or simply giving thanks, the focus of true worship is always the same:

> God has done great things for us!
> God is doing great things for us!
> God will do great things for us!
> Now let's celebrate!

Worship Is Doing Our Thing

A word of caution is in order. If worship becomes a one-man show—the minister doing it all—that kills off celebration. The liturgy, however it's done (whether in a free or formal style), is always "the people's work," or it isn't really worship. That is why both the Old and New Testaments speak of the People of God as priests. We are the ones who are called as a matter of daily practice to "offer up a sacrifice of praise to God, that is, the fruit of lips that acknowledge his name" (Hebrews 13:15). So Paul counsels one congregation to come prepared when they gather for worship to get in on the act and do their thing. "When you come together, each has a hymn, a lesson, a revelation. . . ." (1 Corinthians 14:26).

If you think of worship as a kind of dramatic production in which one has a role to play, it might help the 11–12 hour on Sunday morning come alive. That's how Sören Kierkegaard described worship in his day, when many churchgoers had become only spectators. In the theater there are three important figures:

> —the actors on stage
> —the audience in the seats
> —the prompter in the wings

People, he said, often think that the pastor is the actor and the congregation the audience that has come to watch a performance. They are either charmed or bored or made angry by the preacher who does his act. But that is not worship. In real worship, these roles are reversed:

—the actors are the people
—the audience is God
—the pastor is only the prompter in the wings

The point he makes is that the congregation is there to do and say what the prompter says in order to become before God what God intends. Try to remember that the next time you attend church. Worship is the work of all the People of God, not of the pastor or choir alone. This will mean, of course, that worship will have to be planned so that all the people can get in on the act.

Worship Is a Happening

The question one often hears asked from someone who missed church last Sunday is: "What did he say?" That is, what was the sermon about? The question should be: "What happened?" Worship really takes place and comes alive only when there is an open, eager attitude that expects something to happen, that expects God to arrive on the scene, to speak his word, and to act in the salvation of souls.

Let's take the sermon. Why does it still occupy such an important place in worship? Is it supposed to be the pastor's point of view on current topics? Is it telling people how to be nice in a bad world? Is it not, rather, the pastor unfolding a segment of Scripture and God using the pastor's words to speak his word to the church? The pastor does not make his words God's word, but if he is faithful to the Scriptures and to the current scene and the people are faithful hearers, then, somehow, the miracle happens. The past becomes here-and-now as Jesus comes again into the midst of man

—sitting with sinners
—feeding the hungry
—stilling the storms
—healing the sick
—driving out the money-changers

—calling the dead to life
—teaching, dying, and rising

If you come to church expecting nothing to happen, you will probably not be disappointed. If you come expecting that God is going to confront you, speak his word to you, do something new for you, then something is bound to happen.

That is what I long for more than anything else when I lead the congregation in worship on a Sunday morning. I know too well the barren stretches where nothing happens. The right words may be spoken and sung, the proper order and decorum observed, but life does not come. And I am a man thirsty for life. That is why I long to hear the glad thunder of our early beginnings, eat anew the crusty loaf of God's word, see the descending dove or the fiery tongues resting upon my people, and why I pray both as I work and worship, "Come, Holy Spirit, come!"

Worship in the Future

Through the help of such communications experts as Marshall McLuhan the church is beginning to do some hard thinking about its worship, particularly as it involves young people. It would be hard to deny the immense religious significance of the communications revolution. For example, when you sit in front of your TV, you are getting a message. You are present in a situation where everything that's happening is right before you and you are involved in it, whether it's in New York, Cairo, Timbuktu, or on the moon. McLuhan says that "the medium is the message." Through TV, radio, tape, and records you have a new way of thinking, a new way of feeling, a new way of being in the world.

If we should take our signals from this media revolution, worship in the future will probably mean—in addition to printed and spoken words—using more dramatic and visual ways of communicating God's Good News by such things as

—processions and parades
—colors and lights
—new songs and sounds
—more films and drama

Perhaps worship of the future will be more like the worship of the ancient People of God, which was not just hearing and speaking but getting all the senses into the action.

Whatever the future brings, however, the content will remain the same—the Good News. The role of the messenger or preacher will remain the same—announcing the Good News. The rhythm of worship will be the same—gathering and scattering. That is, we gather in the church building so that we can go out to do the work of God in the classroom, on the football field, at home, in the suburbs or ghetto, giving God our bodies to be his body in the world.

Prayer

God, it is great to be here in church again. Fill every minute of this hour with your presence. Let every note of music, every word of Scripture, every prayer, every offering of money, every part of the sermon be alive with your Spirit. But make this hour special only to remind us that you are present in every hour, that your voice can be heard in every moment, in every day, in every place—if we are tuned in. And when we are tempted to forget, remind us again that in whatever we do in word, thought, or deed, we are called to celebrate you, the true and living God, our God. Amen.

Some Things To Do

1. Read the following: Isaiah 1:10–20, 6:1–8; and 2 Corinthians 14:26–33. Then select *one* of these passages and summarize in an essay what you think it is saying about true worship.

2. Look at this definition of worship: ". . . to worship is to quicken the mind with the truth of God, to purge the imagination by the beauty of God, to open the heart to the love of God, to devote the will to the purpose of God" (William Temple). Then write a paragraph on each of these two questions: (a) What would be the effect on the Christian faith in your community if services of worship were outlawed? (b) Is there a connection between the hymns we sing, the sermons we hear, the prayers we pray, and the sort of persons we become?

3. Read Psalm 95:1–7 and answer the following questions:

   a. In the first four lines (verses 1 and 2), how does the leader of worship invite us to praise God?

   b. What is the attitude or feeling expressed by joining in an act of praise?

   c. In verses 3 to 5, what reasons does the leader of worship give for praising God?

   d. In verse 6, what form of worship does he suggest? Why?

   e. Why do you think the leader of worship uses the figure of sheep and shepherd?

4. As a special project the pastor may wish to appoint a committee from the class to work together in preparing an order of worship that teenagers would consider ideal.

5. Prepare a report on the Christian Year; tell how it originated and what the various seasons and days mean. Or report on the colors of the Christian Year; if your church uses different colors on the pulpit, lectern, or communion table, tell how these colors are visual reminders of the great themes of the gospel as they are celebrated.

6. Make a colorful banner out of cloth, using historic or contemporary symbols or scriptural themes or quotations of great Christians. Perhaps these could be used in public worship.

7. Take notes on next Sunday's sermon and prepare to discuss it in class. Here is an outline which may help you to listen more carefully to the sermon and to get more out of it. You may wish to use this outline in taking notes:

   a. Sermon title and date

   b. Scripture lesson or lessons

   c. Theme of the sermon (what the sermon is about)

   d. Illustrations

   e. What did the sermon teach you?

   f. What did the sermon ask you to do?

   g. What questions did it raise for you?

   h. How did it bring Christ to you?

8. You may wish to discuss some of the following subjects relating to worship in your congregation:

   a. Discuss with your pastor how he goes about preparing the sermon.

   b. How does the architecture of your church building and the arrangement of pulpit, lectern, communion table, and baptismal font express the congregation's understanding of its faith and worship?

   c. Do you think worship needs to have a certain form or structure, or should it be completely spontaneous?

   d. Discuss the meaning of each part of your Sunday morning service as it is printed in the bulletin. Is there anything you would like to see altered?

   e. Discuss with your pastor how the special services of the church such as weddings and funerals are conducted. How do they express Christian meanings, and why should they be occasions of worship by the entire congregation?

   f. Do you think worship should celebrate not only God's presence in past events but in current events also—for example, the birth of a baby, a scientific discovery, a decision of the United Nations or of our national government which benefits mankind?

MEMORY WORK

What is prayer?

Prayer is speaking and listening to God, lifting up our hearts to him in adoration and thanksgiving, confessing our sins, seeking his help for ourselves and others, and waiting expectantly on him.

"Truly, truly, I say to you, if you ask anything of the Father, he will give it to you in my name. Hitherto you have asked nothing in my name; ask, and you will receive, that your joy may be full" (*John 16:23, 24*).

Photo by Thomas Medcalf

22

Go Forth into the World

A People Scattered

SOMETIMES TV COMMERCIALS are better than the programs. I recall one of those thirty-second masterpieces that aimed at extolling the unparalleled worth of "Hush-Puppies." There were feet of all kinds and in all circumstances giving evidence of faithful service in spite of the bulk they carried around and the abuse they were called upon to absorb. Then a voice said something like this:

> "Just think if you didn't have feet. Your socks would come clear up to your knees."

Your Feet

Stop for a moment and look at your feet. Think of the reasons you have for appreciating them. Your feet

—take you from place to place
—help you participate in athletics
—make all kinds of fun possible
—contribute to the economy via the shoe industry.

You need only to see a crippled child to know that the ability to walk and to run is a great gift.

Your Feet and Worship

Often we fail to see the real value of worship and need to be reminded of its importance just as we need to be reminded of the importance of being able to walk and run. Worship can be a kind of pious nod to God on Sunday, taking us nowhere, but it can also be a rich and creative experience.

True worship will get into our feet and carry us out into the world as the People of God. Like feet, worship will

—carry us along
—get us through the hard places
—give us strength to stand alone
—take us where we are most needed

That is why the service of worship in many churches concludes with a charge given by the pastor:

> Go forth into the world in peace; be of good courage; hold fast that which is good; render to no man evil for evil; strengthen the fainthearted; support the weak, help the afflicted; honor all men; love and serve the Lord, rejoicing in the power of the Holy Spirit. The grace of the Lord Jesus Christ and the love of God and the fellowship of the Holy Spirit be with you all. Amen.[1]

In other words, now that you have heard God's Word, get out there. Let your feet start moving in a new direction. Continue what you have begun here. Your worship is not for socks but for feet that take you back to your everyday world. For you this means

—the classroom
—the laboratory
—gym
—drive-in
—pizza shop
—home

What happens in the service must affect what happens on the outside, in the service that never ends.

You Are Held Responsible

That's why the final question we are considering now puts the two words together:

"Do you promise to join us in *worship* and *service* . . . ?"

You get the feeling that not just anything goes. Not just any kind of haphazard behavior entitles you to belong to the church. The church is making some rather specific

---

[1] *The Book of Common Worship,* (Philadelphia, Westminster Press, 1966), p. 33.

demands for which it intends to hold you responsible.

What are these demands? What does the church actually expect of you? It is clear what the church expects by the first part of the question about worship:

> *Minimal requirement:* that your feet start moving in the direction of the church building on Sunday morning where you are present as a physical body occupying space in a pew.
>
> *Maximum requirement:* that you be present not simply as a genetic package but as the whole you, praising God "with heart and hand and voices."

The other part of the question about service is less clear. What does the church expect of you here?

God's People Now

The question is not: "Will you help the church do this and that?" but "Will you help us be the church?" When you confess Jesus as Savior and Lord, you are the laity (literally, members of the *laos*, the People of God). You have something special to give which the church needs if it is to carry out its mission effectively. In so doing, you discover who you are.

Unfortunately, it sometimes happens that teenagers feel or are made to feel that they don't really count. I've heard it put like this:

> "We're only second-rate members or maybe even third-rate. We can't really influence anything. Because they pay the bills, the adults make all the decisions in the church. On Youth Sunday, they tell us how great we are and speak about us as the church of tomorrow. That's not what we want now."

But things are changing. Whether in the church or in politics or in education, young people are making themselves heard. This is good!

For Adults

Adults need to know that when we affirm that the church is the People of God that includes teenagers as well as grownups. Young people who have taken a stand for Christ need to be taken seriously as God's People now, not ten years from now. Those who call the shots need to make some room for teenagers in the way the church is organized. They need to give every opportunity for service based not on age but on gifts; not on personality but on conviction; not on experience alone but on commitment. According to the New Testament, every Christian has something to bring to the whole body to help it carry out its mission to the world. Rather than simply planning for you—or ignoring you—the older laity needs to accept you and challenge you to keep your feet moving now.

For Teenagers

As teenagers you need to use the power you have as the younger laity to show adults that you mean business. This might mean

—asking questions
—finding out what's going on
—speaking out
—voting in congregational meetings
—doing something when asked.

You will also need to listen and learn from the experience of the older laity. But remember that you are God's People now.

God's People in the World

You are also the laity, God's People, within the framework of life as you are experiencing it now. Most of your time, obviously, is not spent in the church building, but you are still a member all the time, wherever you go. The real test of your worship in the church building comes not where prayers are spoken, hymns sung, the Scriptures read, and sermons preached but in the direction your feet take in such spots as these:

—where kids are being shunned
—where teachers are abused
—where answers are being exchanged in exams
—wherever life is lived out.

This is where you must make a choice: taking the easy way out by conforming to the status quo or establishing your identity as one of God's People. If you don't do it in the situation in which you find yourself right now, the chances are that you won't be doing it when you face big decisions in the future.

Your Life Work

Believe it or not, the church is also thinking of service in terms of your life work, how you spend your life. School doesn't last forever. Before you know it, the day will come when you will need to decide what you are going to do. How do you go about making up your mind on a question as big as that? Many young people make choices on such dubious grounds as

—"This job was the first chance I got."
—"I saw a 'help-wanted' ad in the paper."
—"Someone at home decided for me."

That's why the church wants you to start thinking about your life work right away, to probe your own feelings and interests as well as to test attitudes that will help you make your choice in a Christian way. By that I mean the church wants you to find a vocation, not simply an occupation or a job.

There is a difference. You may choose an occupation or job apart from any reference to God's purpose for your life.

But with a vocation it's different. You must discover it or let it discover you. We might put it like this:

—God has a purpose for you
—God calls you to serve that purpose
—God will enable you to get the job done.

Your vocation is your response to Jesus' call, "Follow me," and as his disciple to do "whatever you do . . . to the glory of God" (1 Corinthians 10:31). It's big enough to catch up your whole life—your leisure time as well as your times of work and worship.

The Giant Switchboard

But how do we find it out? One of the biggest problems at any age is deciding just how or where we should spend our lives. If we are interested in meeting human needs, our dilemma might be described like this:

> Imagine yourself sitting behind a giant switchboard with a vast, complicated communications network at your disposal. All kinds of calls are coming in. Some you can handle easily. Others you can ignore or pass on to someone else. But still others create a difficulty. They represent real emergencies. Yet you know that there are only a few to which you can give any prolonged personal care. Nevertheless, you have to decide what calls you can answer, where you can invest your time, energy, and money.[2]

As one of God's People, you know you are here for a purpose: to do his work, to fulfill his purposes for mankind. But the dilemma remains. You will need to evaluate and reflect on the calls coming through on your switchboard and what you know about yourself. No one can be mechanically routed into his vocation by a computer. The human element which is you is indispensable in choosing

---

[2] This image is employed by Harvey Cox in *The Secular City*, Chapter 2.

your life work. Though a machine can "think" or analyze data, it cannot worship or know itself as called by God to serve others. But to help yourself in your dilemma you might try asking such questions as these:

—How do you feel about a certain kind of work? Does it excite you, capture your imagination?
—Does it make use of your talents or abilities?
—Can you imagine how it would help you provide a service people really need?
—Is it the kind of job that makes you want to ask: "What's in it for me?" or the kind that makes you want to ask: "Is this what God wants?"
—Does it help build understanding and enable you to respect all people as children of God?
—Is it the kind of work that provides an opportunity for Christian witness?

God's call sent first-century Christians right into the heart of the world's agonies and struggles. His call to you might mean something similar. But if it's where he wants you, you'll get a kick out of it and a sense of accomplishment. Incidentally, the church doesn't apologize one minute for asking you to consider a special kind of service to your fellow men:

teaching
preaching
medical service
social work
short-term missions, etc.

In fact, the church would like you to consider these kinds of vocations first, not because they are more important than others but because the calls coming in on the giant "switchboard" are so much more urgent for the kinds of help these vocations offer.

"And Now Concerning the Collection"

There is one other thing hooked up with worship and service in this final question: "Do you promise . . . to give regularly of your substance . . . ?" (that is, your money).

I can almost hear your reaction: "Who me?" Yes, you! You have money, some at least, whether it's an allowance or money from an after-school job. When you join the church, you are asked to decide what part of it belongs to God.

You might think of it like this. When you give money to God's work, it is very much like buying your parents a present out of the allowance they have given you. That's where giving begins: we are giving back a part of something that belongs to God, something he freely shares with us as his People. No one says you have to give. Neither God nor the church demand your money. It's not like paying income tax. It's just that everything belongs to God, including our money, even if it's only pocket money.

But the reason for our giving lies deeper than this. When one of my children gives me a Christmas present, I hope it's not because he feels he has to but because he wants to do so to show his love for me. Giving is Christian only when it is done out of sheer gratitude for God's gift, Jesus Christ, "his gift beyond words" (2 Corinthians 9:15, *New English Bible*). If that can be grasped and acted upon, we should be well on the way to deciding how much to give.

Many churches encourage the practice of tithing as a business-like way of determining how much one should give. (A tithe is a dime out of every dollar you earn or receive.) What is more important however is your willingness to give joyously out of what you have—not money only but your time, talents, bodies, everything. Your money—both what you give and what you spend or keep—tells God what you value most, what you think of the mission of the church, perhaps even what you think of him.

Putting whatever you own at God's disposal is a way to prevent being overrun by socks, that is, putting feet to your worship to serve "the work of the gospel as carried on by this church and the denomination to which it belongs."

Prayer

> I am only one—but I am one.
> I can count—
> As much as one can count.
> No one can count more.
> I can cast one vote,
> . . . can set one example,
> . . . fill one seat,
> . . . add support,
> encouragement, effort.
> I can deposit one life
> And bear dividends for God.
> And by the divine arithmetic
> Of God's purpose and plan
> My life joined to other lives,
> Invested by God in his work,
> Brings rich returns
> . . . a hundredfold.
> Here is my life, O God—
> Add to it other lives
> Multiply it by thy power,
> . . . Make it count.
>   —Oliver de W. Cummings [3]

Some Things To Do

1. Read 1 Corinthians 13 (preferably from the Phillips translation or the New English Bible), and write an essay on how worship, according to this chapter, might affect your life as a student. Try to give at least three specific examples.

2. Make a switchboard of cardboard or heavy paper. Then (a) write on slips of paper the names of persons, groups, and causes which you are given opportunity to support either

---

[3] "Young People," January 3, 1960, published by the American Baptist Board of Education and Publication.

through time or money or effort. Include as many as you can. You may prefer to use snapshots or pictures from magazines. (b) Paste these slips of paper or pictures on your switchboard. (c) Circle in red those that require the most of your personal concern; in yellow those you can give only passing concern; in blue those you must ignore; in green those you would like to do something about in your lifework. It is important to be honest and certain that what you circle is true to your use of time, money, or energy.

3. Choose one of these quotations and tell how it might be related to your own life and that of your own congregation:

a. *On worship and service:* " 'Serve the Lord with gladness! Come into his presence with singing' we read before a cultic worship service. But this is the wrong time to read it; instead, it should be read before we go out from the worship service. 'Serve the Lord with gladness' does not mean a cultic activity but service in the literal sense." [4]

b. *On vocation:* "We had to learn ourselves and furthermore, we had to teach the despairing men (imprisoned in a concentration camp during World War II), that it did not really matter what we expected from life, but rather what life expected from us. We needed to stop asking about the meaning of life, and instead to think of ourselves as those who were being questioned by life—daily and hourly. Our answer must consist, not in talk and meditation, but in right action and in right conduct. Life ultimately means taking the responsibility to find the right answer to its problems and to fulfil the tasks which it constantly sets for each individual." [5]

c. *On Christian witness:* ". . . out of missionary China comes the story of the evangelists who laid aside their Bibles in a famine and concentrated on issuing rice to enormous queues of starving men. It was disturbing on the first day that about every seventh suppliant, his bowl filled, demanded of the servers that they should tell him about Jesus. Better organized the next day they had a tent behind the open-air counter with the title 'Evangelist' pinned to its door flap. As the suppliants began again to say, 'Sir, we

---

[4] Harvey Cox, *God's Revolution and Man's Responsibility*, (Judson Press, 1965), p. 84.
[5] *Man's Search for Meaning, op. cit.,* p. 77.

would see Jesus,' the server brightly pointed them to the evangelist's tent. But without exception the inquirers remonstrated, 'We do not want to hear about Him from the man in the tent but from you who so costingly care." [6]

4. Be prepared to discuss the following:

a. If your house were on fire and you could rescue five things, what would they be? Why these things?

b. Joseph Fletcher says: "Taxation is stewardship." Do you agree?

c. Do you think your church takes its teenagers seriously? Is the program of your youth organization an adequate expression of service for teenagers as the younger laity? Do you think your involvement is too segregated from adults or not segregated enough?

d. Do you think Christians can witness to their faith by becoming involved in making necessary changes in our society to relieve the suffering of people?

e. What proportion of a teenager's money do you think should be given to the church?

---

[6] Sara Little, *Youth, World and Church*, (John Knox Press, 1968), pp. 57–58. Quoted from *Only One Way Left*, George MacLeod.

MEMORY WORK

What is the meaning of death?

Death means that our earthly life will come to an end and that we must all give an account of our lives before the judgment seat of Christ.

"For we must all appear before the judgment seat of Christ, so that each one may receive good or evil, according to what he has done in the body" (*2 Corinthians 5:10*).

Photos from *By One Spirit*, by Karl A. Olsson.
Published by Covenant Press

23

Who
Are We?

Covenant Companions

Sunday	*Deuteronomy 7:6–11* Out of Bondage
Monday	*Deuteronomy 10:12–22* Your God
Tuesday	*Jeremiah 31:31–34* A New Covenant
Wednesday	*2 Corinthians 5:16–21* A New Creation
Thursday	*Isaiah 43:8–13* God's Witnesses
Friday	*2 Timothy 1:1–7* A Great Heritage
Saturday	*Psalm 119:57–64* Companion of All

WHEN YOU JOIN the church and say "I do" to all of these promises, it's important to remember that you don't belong only to that church down the street or across town or in the country—your church. You also belong to the church that consists of all the People of God who have ever lived and are living, "the Church as we see her spread out through all time and space and rooted in eternity, terrible as an army with banners" (C. S. Lewis). That's what the old catechism had in mind when it said:

> "There is only one Christian Church: It includes all the redeemed in heaven and on earth."

If you stop and think about it, that's really quite breathtaking, isn't it? That's probably how it looks through God's eyes—one People stretching clear back to the ancient patriarchs, and each denomination and local congregation an outpost of that vast company, one cell in the total body. It's enough to make your head swim.

The Church Where You Are

But the way the last question is put is terribly down to earth.

> "Do you promise to join us in worship and service and to give regularly to the work of the gospel as carried on by this church and the denomination to which it belongs?"

That doesn't leave any loop-holes. It says we get in touch with the People of God and wade into this vast stream of history at one particular place. In other words, unless you enter some nucleus of the People of God right where you are, you are in danger of becoming something like a confirmed bachelor who waxes eloquent on the virtues of marriage but who never gets around to committing himself to one girl.

A Personal Word

The starting point for my Christian life began at a particular address, in a rather ugly building, in a form of service not particularly exciting, with ordinary people, and with things you could see and touch. Behind and within this particular congregation and its way of doing things, working through it and often in spite of it, was something else: the calling of Almighty God. I can never be grateful enough for the one place where I got tuned in with the People of God and where Christ became present and real to me.

Special Memories

We discovered earlier that we have lots of memories we share with all the People of God:

—the history of the Jews in our history
—the history of Jesus Christ in our history
—the history of the early Church in our history
—the history of the martyrs in our history, and so on and on.

But when you join the Covenant Church, you discover some special memories you don't find anywhere else. That doesn't mean they are better than the memories other Christians have. It simply means that by God's grace this is who *we* are. Just as your family has its treasury of stories and anecdotes that are frequently retold and celebrated on special occasions, thereby giving our family its special identity, so it is with the Covenant Church. We have our memories that help us to understand who we are.

Inner History

History can provide part of the answer. We need the facts of when and how it all began. But with the facts we need something else: history not after the flesh (facts only), but history after the spirit (meanings), what has become a part of our lives as selves.

Poetry helps us to think feelingly about who we are. For example, Dr. Karl Olsson's poem in his monumental history of the Covenant Church, *By One Spirit*, lets history happen for us. You sense the character and mood of the founding fathers in a way that facts alone cannot convey.

> Out of the east, hulks of men wearing homespun
> And heavy shoes;
> With brass snuff boxes;
> With something rigid behind the Swedish steel of their
>   eyes;
> Men with bronze beards over barrel chests,
> And loud voices seldom heard.
>
> Out of the east little, sad women;
> With heaven-hymns in their minds;
> Remembering the prayer meeting in the school house
>   among the birches,
> Remembering dark bread and patched trousers;
> Holding children against mute breasts.
>
> Out of the east little twists of memories;
> Of heather moors in blossom,
> Of hills holding out the eyes of a world.
>
> Out of the east, great desires
> In the brains of men with bronze beards:
> In the hearts of the women thinking of heaven-hymns.
>
> Out of the east, a Great Ambition.[1]

Who were these people from the east? If we are to explain who we are as Covenanters, we must know something about who they were.

Two Homes

The poem indicates that these people who came to America were a wistful people who looked in two directions—home to Sweden and home to heaven. They lived and worked in the tension of being aliens and pilgrims.

---

[1] Karl A. Olsson, *By One Spirit,* (Chicago, Covenant Press, 1962), p. 312.

But they were also people of another tension which, I believe, provides a significant clue as to who we are:

> There is in our tradition the uniqueness, experienced at the beginning of our church, of having two homes: church and conventicle.[2]

What does this mean? Just as the early church had two places of worship—the Temple and private homes—so we had two places of worship—the Lutheran State Church of Sweden and private homes. The meetings in homes were sometimes called "conventicles." Later these gatherings led to "mission houses" and finally to church buildings. Though the house-meetings tended to become the norm or pattern for church life here in America, the tension of two places of worship accounts in large measure for the often surprising variety of the people called Covenanters.

The House-Meeting

What were these informal gatherings in the homes of believers like? There was a great deal of variety in these meetings, but they all had certain things in common:

1. The fellowship was free and open. There were no bulletins to tell what came next and no clergy leading in worship—not because these things were wrong but because they were unnecessary. What mattered was sharing life in Christ with each other, and, in so doing, experiencing the fellowship of the Spirit. What furthered that life was important above everything else.

2. The reading of the Bible as a devotional book. They were called "readers" not so much in the sense that they were seeking for a correct theology but in the sense that they were seeking for peace with God. The purpose of the house-meeting was to draw out the meaning of the Bible, not for teaching or even Bible study but for letting the Bible question, evaluate, and judge their life as believers.

---

[2] C. John Weborg, "Some Reflections on Church Life: Pietistic Concerns," *Covenant Quarterly*, XXI, No. 3 (August, 1963), p. 3.

3. The confession of sins. Such reading of the Bible called for self-examination and the honest confession of sins. They might recall experiences out of their daily life and work and bring them up for group discussion as they listened together for God's personal word. In an atmosphere of honesty and acceptance, where men were not afraid to admit they were sinners, they were able to receive healing and forgiveness. The word of confession from one would call forth the same in another. So the house-meeting breathed the atmosphere of conversion and of new life.

4. Laymen had a place of importance. The early preachers were nearly all laymen—tailors, blacksmiths, shoemakers, and farmers. In the parish church they had to sit in silence; in the house-meeting, they were free to speak and to pray. This was especially true of the gifted person who was clever with words. Because there was the ring of authority—or at least originality—in what he said, he assumed a special place of leadership. Where there was a sermon, its purpose was to help people decide to follow Christ.

5. Songs were of the folk type. Nothing seems to have brought them closer to fellowship with Christ than the singing of hymns. But these were not the same kind of hymns they sang in church. They were the kind that could be accompanied on the guitar. They were also the kind that came from the heart of the people.

The purpose of these house-meetings was not to compete with the established church. It was, rather, to promote a genuine Christian life, one that was not phoney but one that could be seen and demonstrated both in personal terms and in their life together. What you did at home or at work was the test of your experience with Christ. Faith without a new life to back it up was dead.

The Church

You can never quite understand these people—and who we are—apart from the churchly tradition they inherited. When these people moved out of the conventicle and began to build mission houses, the sense of beauty and order in worship seemed at times almost absent. It was like the house-meeting where the fellowship was free and informal, often folksy. But these people were also Lutherans. As Dr. Olsson points out:

> . . . a group of people disciplined by generations of instruction and worship in the Lutheran church and accustomed to orderliness of life within that communion could not, however sudden or thorough-going their personal encounter with Christ, be expected to become spiritual anarchists. . . . In the public schools the children of Mission Friends (the nickname for early Covenanters) were instructed daily in the Shorter Catechism of Luther. They sang Lutheran psalms and heard Lutheran prayers. Most of them were confirmed by Lutheran pastors. . . . They all had Luther's Shorter Catechism and the hymns and the prayers in their blood.[3]

Though they may have reacted against the churchly, yet it formed their life and thought in such ways as these:

1. They understood the Word and sacraments as means of grace largely in Lutheran terms.
2. They regarded confirmation as a necessary part of learning the Faith and growing up in the Christian life, with Luther's Shorter Catechism as the core of instruction.
3. They kept the practice of the Christian Year in preaching so that the whole gospel would be set forth.
4. They kept alive an appreciation for the chorale tradition of church music. In the hymnal of the Covenant Church you can observe the music of the house-meeting standing along-side the stately music of the church.
5. They retained respect for a trained and ordained ministry.

---

[3] Karl A. Olsson, "Covenant Beginnings: Communal," *Covenant Quarterly*, XIII, No. 3 (August, 1953), pp. 76 and 78.

These two homes in which we had our origins have shaped, in large measure, what we are today. Both are necessary. The spirit of the house-meeting serves to keep alive a concern for a real Christian life as well as preserving an honest, compassionate life together. The spirit of the churchly serves to keep us in the main currents of historic Christianity with its emphasis on the given means of grace: the Word and the sacraments. One focuses on life and freedom in the Spirit; the other, on order and history. Both are the heritage of those people from the east.

Life in Christ

What brought these two homes together was life and freedom in Christ. Knowing Christ gave one the freedom to accept all that served this life and freedom to reject all that seemed to hinder it. When some confirmation students were asked what they thought best characterized the Covenant Church and what they most wanted it to become in the future, these were some of their answers:

—a group of people open to the future
—a group of people awake to the needs of the world
—a group of people who care about one another
—a group of people who are listening to the Bible
—a group of people who are celebrating

Actually, what those teenagers were expressing is very close to what one of our founding fathers, David Nyvall, called "Covenant Ideals." [4] Using the language of the teenagers, but filling in with Nyvall's vision, we have this picture of the church of tomorrow.

---

[4] David Nyvall and Karl A. Olson, *The Evangelical Covenant Church,* (Chicago, Covenant Press, 1954), Chapter Seven.

Open to the Future

We want to be a people who are open, able to listen to young people and to discover the next generation—its speech and its soul. We don't claim to know all the answers, but we are trying to ask the right questions and to give people freedom to work out the answers. If we take this seriously, it will mean taking some risks, doing some experimenting, making some changes, looking ahead.

Awake to the Needs of the World

We want to be what our early name suggests—"Mission Friends"—which will mean fulfilling our mission wherever we find it. Our schools, hospitals, retirement homes, Christian education programs, missions at home and throughout the world are essential. These are the ways by which our spiritual goals are given substance.

Caring About One Another

Who are the happiest kids you know? Those who are free from all responsibility or those who are free to care? We are not simply free from something or someone; we are called by Christ to be free to be what we are, to do and to act. This is not something we have attained or decided that sets us apart from others; it is, rather, a way of pointing to what God's grace gives and does. We are free to be obedient, free to care.

Listening to the Bible

The basis of our life together is not a creed which is final in and of itself. It is faith in a living Person, Jesus Christ, in all that he is and in all that he came to do for us. The Bible is the book that points us to him, to the life he came to give us. Creeds have a teaching value. As Nyvall suggested, they are like dippers, whereas the New Testament is like the well. Why be satisfied with what you can take from the dipper when you have the whole well? Here is where our life is found. When we meditate on it, ponder it in our hearts, study it, apply it to ourselves, then and only then does it become a life-giving power.

Celebrating

David Nyvall didn't use the word, but he breathed its spirit. To be born into freedom is to live out one's day in celebrating God's grace in Christ. It is to be "the church of the free," free to proceed on the errands of mercy to which we have been sent, free to love without counting the cost, free to allow ourselves to be carried by this freedom, free to give whatever one is and has in the assurance that the Spirit will make us more than adequate to meet the need. Such freedom enables us to celebrate! To celebrate God's grace! To celebrate who we are!

Though we do not yet see all of these ideals taking form in our Covenant, the fact remains that they are there as a part of that inheritance we have been given. Whatever the future brings to our church, we can be grateful for the special memories that are ours. As you join a Covenant congregation, you can help us be what we are called to be —the pilgrim People of God moving out through history toward a glorious destiny!

Prayer

> Savior, in Thy love abiding
> Keep me with Thy tender care;
> Through Thy Spirit's gentle guiding
> Save me from each tempting snare.
>
> Speak Thy words of inspiration
> When I fail to see Thy will,
> Grant in grace Thy consolation,
> Faith and hope and love instill.
>
> On the unknown path before me
> Guide me with Thy mighty hand.

Should I faint and fall, restore me;
Through all perils help me stand.

Cast Thy mantle fair around me,
Draw me closer to Thy heart;
When Thy peace and joy surround me
Pains and sorrows all depart.

Unto Thee my will is yielded,
Mold it to conform to Thine.
By Thy grace and mercy shielded,
Help me live a life divine. Amen.
—Selma Lagerström

Some Things To Do

1. In the light of this year's confirmation study and this chapter on the Covenant Church, write an essay on the theme: How do you feel you can help the church be more obedient to Christ? Or you might prefer this topic: How does the church help you to understand who you are?

2. Take *one* of the following hymns and rewrite it, using your own words and ideas:

   Praise the Lord, Each Tribe and Nation
   Out of My Bondage, Sorrow and Night
   I Sing with Joy and Gladness

3. Using resources in the church library, report on *one* of the following:

   a. a Covenant mission field

   b. a Covenant missionary—Peter Matson, or Dr. Paul Carlson, or someone you know personally

   c. a Covenant institution such as North Park College and Theological Seminary, Swedish Covenant Hospital, or a Covenant retirement home

   d. how the Covenant Church is organized or how your local congregation is organized

4. Be prepared to discuss the following questions:

a. Is it possible to make an idol out of a congregation or a denomination?

b. What would you say to a person who says he does not believe in missions?

c. If you were called to be a missionary, in what country would you like to serve?

d. What should our attitude be toward other Christian churches?

You might wish to use this statement as a basis for your discussion:

"As though in preparation for such a time as this, God has been building up a Christian fellowship which now extends into almost every nation, and binds citizens of them all together in true unity and mutual love. No human agency has planned this. It is the result of the great missionary enterprise of the last hundred and fifty years. . . . Almost incidentally the great world-fellowship has arisen; it is the great new fact of our era. . . . Here is one great ground of hope for the coming days—this world-wide Christian fellowship, this ecumenical movement, as it is often called. . . . It is of urgent importance that we become aware of it, that we further it in every way open to us, and that through it we take our part in providing for the spirit of Christ the agency by which he may transform the world." [5]

[5] William Temple, *The Church Looks Foreward*, (Macmillan Co., 1944), pp. 2, 3, 4.

MEMORY WORK

What does the Bible teach about the final judgment?

The Bible teaches, concerning the final judgment, that Christ as king and judge shall separate the righteous from the unrighteous. The righteous will live forever with God and his people, and the unrighteous will be separated forever from the presence of God.

"Do not marvel at this; for the hour is coming when all who are in the tombs will hear his voice and come forth, those who have done good, to the resurrection of life, and those who have done evil, to the resurrection of judgment" (*John* 5:28, 29).

24

Come, Lord Jesus!

People on the Way

Sunday	*Hebrews 11:13–16* Seeking Something Better
Monday	*Philippians 3:12–16* Eager for What's Ahead
Tuesday	*2 Peter 3:8–13* If the World Blows Up
Wednesday	*1 Corinthians 15:20–28* The Final Curtain
Thursday	*1 Corinthians 15:50–58* Victory in Christ
Friday	*Matthew 25:31–46* Some Big Surprises
Saturday	*1 John 3:1–3* Becoming Like Christ

Now THAT YOU ARE COMING to the end of your confirmation study, and, hopefully, to the beginning of your own personal commitment to the life and work of the People of God in the world, let's take a final look at the discipline you accept when you join this community. Your pastor will ask:

> "Do you believe the Bible to be the Word of God and the only perfect rule for faith, doctrine, and conduct?"

The church expects you to have some definite Christian convictions to shape your style of life.

> "Do you confess Jesus Christ as your Savior and Lord?"

The church expects you to make it a matter of public record that your primary loyalty is to this Person.

> "Do you purpose to remain steadfast in the faith unto the end, and as a true follower of Jesus Christ to walk in newness of life?"

The church expects you to commit yourself to the long haul of Christian living.

> "Do you promise in watchfulness and prayer to diligently use the Word of God and the Holy Sacraments?"

The church expects you to make use of the daily rations that God provides to keep his People moving out into the world in service.

> "Do you promise to join us in worship and service and to give regularly of your substance for the work of the gospel as carried on by this church and the denomination to which it belongs?"

The church expects you to be a flesh-and-blood Christian who is present and available for front-line duty.

When You Say "I Do"

You don't have to say "I do" to any of these questions any more than you have to be confirmed. In fact, if you can't say it and mean it, then don't fake it. Give yourself time so that when you say "I do" you and everyone else will know for certain that your belonging to the People of God is no empty gesture but is your way of deciding who you are and what you want to become. No half-way commitment will do.

After you say "I do," the pastor will say:

> "We, the members of this congregation, welcome you with joy into our communion and fellowship. We pledge to you our affection, our help, and our prayers, that you with us may evermore increase in the knowledge and love of God. As an expression of our welcome and in token of our brotherly love, I now give you the right hand of fellowship."

Then he will most likely give your hand a good, firm shake (an old custom that goes back to the early church) which intends to say, "Glad to have you along, pilgrim!"

A Christian Never Graduates

Joining the People of God, however, is not like getting a diploma so that you can say: "See, I made it. I've arrived!" any more than being confirmed is like graduation. In fact, a Christian never graduates from the need to "evermore increase in the knowledge and love of God," as the *Book of Worship* says. When you become a member of the People of God, you will often look at yourself—your weakness, failure, stubborness, few talents—and say:

> "Who me? the church? It was a whole lot easier when I could pick out the faults of the church and say 'They.' Now I have to say 'We.'"

But you will be among people who feel just the same way you do, yet say, in spite of their failures or even their achievements:

> "One thing I do, forgetting what lies behind and straining forward to what lies ahead, I press on toward the goal. . . ."
>
> (Philippians 3:13,14).

A Pilgrim People

The word "pilgrim" best describes the church as a people on the move—a people grateful for its memories of God's deeds in the past but constantly looking toward the future with hopeful expectation. In the Acts of the Apostles the earliest Christians were referred to as those "who followed the new way" (Acts 9:2, *New English Bible*). The phrase suggests several things:

—followers of Jesus, who called himself "the Way"
—pilgrims who could never live settled lives since they were on the road leading to God's Kingdom
—people who were not just catching up or keeping pace but were pioneers out in front of the rest, cutting some new paths for the rest of humanity.

Have you noticed how many of the hymns we sing convey this notion of the pilgrimage of God's People advancing through darkness and storm toward the Promised Land?

> Chosen seed and Zion's children,
> Ransomed from eternal wrath,
> Traveling to the heav'nly Canaan,
> On a rough and thorny path.

Or

> Through the night of doubt and sorrow
> Onward goes the pilgrim band,

>Singing songs of expectation,
>Marching to the promised land.

Or

>Guide me, O Thou great Jehovah,
>Pilgrim through this barren land.

Or

>As pilgrims in this world where life is fleeting,
>We journey on to meet our dearest Friend.

The Long Trek

As you look back over your confirmation studies, I hope you begin to feel something of the excitement that comes in the discovery that the story of the ancient People of God —Israel—continued in the story of the new People of God —the Church—is still being written in 19__ (you fill in the date) by ordinary people like you and me. When you say "I do," you become part of the same pilgrim people as Abraham and Moses and all the rest of the patriarchs, apostles, prophets, and redeemed sinners who are seeking "the reconciliation of all things in heaven and on earth."

No, you're not Abraham. Nor am I. Most likely you have never heard a divine command that changed your name or home. Nor are you Moses. Chances are you have never seen a burning bush, led slaves out of captivity, or heard God speak on the top of a mountain. But if you choose to be, you can be part of that same stream of history-making You believe what they believed—not so well, perhaps, but you are trying nevertheless to listen to the same call they heard, to respond by breaking out of your self-centered existence, and to start out on a risky adventure that is going somewhcre. I hope you will accept a place for yourself among this pilgrim People of God and start moving.

What's Coming?

But do you ever wonder where it's all going to end? The world is in quite a mess! What if it all blows up? Ever since the atom bomb exploded over Hiroshima, people have been conscious of the possibility of a sudden end to everything. And what's ahead for the church? More strife and division? Then, too, do you ever think about what's ahead for you? Do you ever wonder about your own death? Asking questions like these, we often feel there must be something more than a huge cemetery and our own tombstone to look forward to!

Thank God, there is! An important part of the kerygma or preaching of the early church was the Good News that

1) in Jesus the Christ the kingdom of God had already begun to come (Acts 2:16;3:18,24)
2) God's full kingdom is not yet perfectly established but the Lord who has begun his rule will come again for the fulfillment of his kingdom (Acts 3:22;10:42).

Consequently, the early Christians faced their times and the future with a wonderful confidence and joy. What made them such a mystery to their contemporaries was that when circumstances were the most depressing they were cheerful. What they had already tasted of God's mercy in Jesus Christ filled them with zest for life and for what God had waiting for them. They lived on tip-toes in expectation that he would soon return. He was just around the corner. Any day the last judgment on evil would take place, and a world of perfect love, service, peace and justice—such as they had seen lived out in Jesus of Nazareth —would be established. So whenever they gathered to break bread and remember him, they would offer the prayer:

"Come, Lord Jesus!"

Significantly, the New Testament ends with the same prayer. It summed up the faith of this waiting, expectant People of God who were ever seeking communion with the coming Lord. If they did not know *what* was coming, they knew *who* was coming.

Triumphant Ending

There are many other images that seek to describe the destination of the journey, such as

Day of the Lord	Last Judgment
New heavens and new earth	World to Come
New Jerusalem	City of God
Resurrection	Life Everlasting

Right now, most images of the life to come don't seem very exciting. Frankly, the thought of playing harps, wearing white robes, and walking on golden streets doesn't excite me much either. What these images mean, however, is another thing. Put as simply as I know how, they tell us that

> History—including the history of the world, the People of God, yours and mine—is going somewhere. It will end triumphantly at his feet. This means then that the Lord is not just a figure of our imagination, but he is really in control of history. As the Negro spiritual says, "He's got the whole world in his hands." And even now he is leading his purposes for all mankind to fulfillment.

That's Good News! But the picture is not all rosy. The kerygma also says:

> "He is the One designated by God as judge of the living and the dead" (Acts 10:42)

That is, you can miss the way, never reach the goal, or become what God created you to be. As one novelist put it:

> Just you wait. Wait for the first quarter-of-an-hour's silence. Then the Word will be heard of men—not the voice they rejected, which spoke so quietly: "I am the Way, the Resurrection, and the Life"—but the voice from the depths: "I am the door forever locked, the road which leads nowhere, the lie, the everlasting dark." [1]

A Parable

For the People of God, however, the destination of the journey promises to be good. That's why traveling with others who share the same hope has its excitement too. Let me try to illustrate how this happy ending lends excitement and joy to the trip we are now on.

> Try thinking of history (including your own) as a drama being played out on the stage of the world. Let's say the drama is a murder-mystery. The opening scene is important because there is a murder that needs to be solved, and there are certain facts of the case we need to know. But it's the final scene when the murderer is caught that determines whether the whole effort makes any sense.

If you are watching the play for the first time, it is the middle part of the drama which is most confusing—that part we are living through right now. The plot is not clear. But now let us suppose you are not a spectator in the drama but an actor. That makes a tremendous difference. For if you know the Playwright who assigns you your part, what character you are supposed to be playing, how you fit into the total picture of what's happening, and above all, where it's all going to come out in the end, then despite the seeming lack of plot in the middle part, you are still certain the play makes sense.

---

[1] George Bernanos, *The Diary of a Country Priest,* (New York, Macmillan Company, 1954 [Image Books]), p. 16.

This is precisely the role of Jesus Christ, who is called "the Alpha" (the beginning) and "the Omega" (the end). He is the Playwright who is directing the drama. Knowing him in the power of his resurrection, we are given the clue to what the end will be like, how we can fill our role in the action. Therefore we can live toward the final curtain with confidence and hope.

The Future Has Already Begun

If we are sure that things will turn out right in the end, it won't mean that we'll start climbing to the mountain tops in white robes waiting for the end, as some have done. Neither will it mean folding our hands, sitting around doing nothing but dreaming of "pie in the sky by and by." Rather, it will mean getting ready for the bright future ahead by beginning to pre-enact it with God's People here and now. That is, we will start practicing our parts in anticipation of the last act when justice will win out, evil and death will be destroyed, and God will be triumphant. In fact, we can actually help God write tomorrow's headlines by launching out in the present toward the goal of the coming kingdom.

During the early part of the sixteenth century, a rumor swept all over Europe that on a certain day the end of the world would come. On the day prior to that date, when many people were in the grips of hysteria and fear, someone asked Martin Luther: "Tell me what you would do today if you were absolutely convinced that tomorrow the world would end." Luther replied: "I would pay my debts and plant an apple tree."

Demonstrating Hope

That's precisely the point!

—If the end means peace and unity, we can start being peace-makers here and now.

—If the end means a new creation, we can start being witnesses to it here and now.

—If the end means "the glorious liberty of the children of God," we can start serving the cause of lesser liberties here and now.

—If the end means a rule of righteousness, we can start becoming politically involved for the sake of righteousness here and now.

—If the end means one People of God, we can start breaking down walls that keep us apart here and now.

—If the end means new heavens and a new earth, we can start planting apple trees in hope of the harvest to come. That is, we can start taking part in the creation of this new order of things.

The pilgrim People of God, at their best, are the pioneers or pace-setters for the rest of the world. As "followers of the new way" they can afford failure and good humor because they know what kind of journey it is they are on and where it leads. And even if they don't always know the right strategy, they nevertheless know they are on the winning team.

Who Are You?

Before we drop the conversation we began together in chapter one, take another look at the "Who am I?" page in your notebook. Would you like to add or subtract anything now that you've had time to think about it? You know at least one thing for certain now—that finding out who you are is not something that suddenly happens. It's more like a life-long business. And in this long, slow, and sometimes agonizing struggle, we all seem like amateurs at times. But take heart! It's reassuring to know that the last entry on this page will not be mine or yours but God's. As one far wiser than this pilgrim once said:

"My dear friends, we are now God's children, but it is not yet clear what we shall become. But this we know, we

shall become like him, because we shall see him as he really is. Everyone who has this hope in Christ keeps himself pure, just as Christ is pure"
(1 John 3:2,3, *Good News for Modern Man*).

I can think of no better way of ending this book than to pray in the spirit of readiness in which I try to live:

"So be it. Come, Lord Jesus!"

Prayer

Dear God, I have come now to the end of my confirmation study. Before I close my book and lay it aside for awhile, I want to thank you for the shafts of light that have shone through the cracks and crevices of my mind and heart

—the majestic sweep of the history of your People through the ages
—the witness to that history in the Bible and the continuing story of the church
—a growing appreciation for flesh and blood people in my congregation who care about me and what happens to me
—the members of my confirmation class and my pastor, whose patience, wisdom, kindness and good humor have shown me that he is a real person.

Most of all, I want to thank you for responding to my deepest needs, fulfilling my innermost longings. I asked for security, and you encompassed me with love. I looked to you for life, and you gave me eternal life. I sought for identity, and you adopted me as your son. To show my thanks, let the vows I speak on Confirmation Day be backed up by a life of true discipleship with your Son, who shows me my deepest reason for being. Keep me tuned-in with him, with you, and with all your People until that day when black, white, yellow, and brown, Jews and Gentiles, Protestants and Catholics will walk hand in hand as brothers, and you will be everything to everyone. Hear this prayer I offer in Jesus' Name. Amen.

Some Things To Do

1. Look up the meaning of the word "pilgrim" in a dictionary. Then do the following: (a) Look up the following references in your Bible and report to the class what the writer is saying about the People of God as sojourners, strangers, and pilgrims.

Exodus 23:9	Acts 7:6
Deuteronomy 23:7	Acts 7:29
Genesis 15:13	Hebrews 11:13
Genesis 23:3, 4	Hebrews 13:14
Psalm 39:12	1 Peter 2:11

   (b) Describe the difficulties some of these people met in their long and dangerous journeys:

   The Vikings
   Columbus
   The first colonists to America
   Daniel Boone
   Lewis and Clark
   The astronauts

   (c) In a brief paragraph describe how salvation is the journey from death to life.

2. Listen to the following two songs from *West Side Story:* (Columbia OS 2070)

   Tony's song: Something's Coming
   Tony and Maria's song: Somewhere

   Then be prepared to respond in class to such questions as these: Is there anything in these selections resembling Christian hope, or is it mere wishful thinking? Where does Christian hope have its roots?

3. Write an essay, using either one of the following quotations as a starter, on how Christ helps us to face the future:

   a. After spending a week working an a poverty-area of our country (Appalachia) one Covenant teenager spoke for the rest of the group when he said to the congregation of his home church:

   "In case you haven't heard, there's a group of young people running around who call themselves the 'Mission Possible' squad. They are a group who, like millions of other young people, believe in the future. But they realize that a bright future requires time and effort *now*. They are the image-changers."

b. On the evening before his assassination (April 3, 1968), Dr. Martin Luther King, Jr. said in his last sermon:

"We've got some difficult days ahead. But it really doesn't matter with me now. Because I've been to the mountaintop. I won't mind. Like anybody, I would like to live a long life. Longevity has its place. But I'm not concerned about that now. I just want to do God's will. And he's allowed me to go up to the mountain. And I've looked over, and I've seen the Promised Land. I may not get there with you, but I want you to know tonight that we as a people will get to the Promised Land. So I'm happy tonight. I'm not fearing any man. Mine eyes have seen the glory of the coming of the Lord." [2]

4. Plan an interview with either a pastor of another Protestant church or a Roman Catholic priest for the purpose of summarizing the views of other Christians on heaven and hell. Your pastor may want to assign members of the class for these interviews.

5. Draw a picture or make a collage or wall-hanging showing Christ leading you on the journey from death to life.

6. Choose one of the following for discussion:

a. "There are only two kinds of people in the end: those who say to God, 'Thy will be done,' and those to whom God says in the end, 'Thy will be done.' All that are in Hell, choose it. Without that self-choice there could be no Hell. No soul that seriously and constantly desires joy will ever miss it. Those who seek find. To those who knock it is opened." [3]

b. "Earthmen will probably complete exploration of the solar system within a hundred years, and scientists hold little hope of finding anywhere in the system conditions suitable for a heaven. Our present knowledge of the physical limits to speed of travel makes planets of stars other

[2] *Time*, April 12, 1968,
[3] C. S. Lewis, *The Great Divorce*, (Macmillan Co., 1962), p. 69.

than the sun seem quite improbable as practical sites for an after-life. In short, our present and anticipated knowledge of scientific facts would seem to eliminate the possibility of heaven as a real place where transformed humans can pursue activities that have any real appeal to us." [4]

c. What do you think of these definitions?
—Heaven is being so close to God that we know and love him perfectly now and always.
—Hell is locking God out forever.
—"Hell is other people."

d. There is an old legend about a saint encountering an angel walking down the road with a torch in one hand and a pail of water in the other. When asked what they were for, he replied: "The torch is to burn down the castles of heaven and the water to put out the flames of hell, and then we shall see who really loves God."

e. Because of the new relationship with God which Christ has opened up to the Christian, he has begun to live eternally now. According to the New Testament, he is experiencing eternal life every moment. If this is true, how would it make a difference in his attitude, behavior, and sense of purpose?

f. "Our congregation is a community of pilgrims on a journey from death to life. By our acts of obedience and faith, we can set up signs here and now for all men to see which point to the coming victory."

[4] "A New Scientific Religion," H. G. MacPherson, *Saturday Review,* Aug. 2, 1969.

MEMORY WORK

What is the Christian hope?

The Christian hope is the assurance that God's purposes for his pilgrim people will end in triumph at the return of Christ, that we shall be raised with him, and that the Lord will reign forever with his church in the age to come.

"In all these things we are more than conquerors through him who loved us. For I am sure that neither death, nor life, nor angels, nor principalities, nor things present, nor things to come, nor powers, nor height, nor depth, nor anything else in all creation, will be able to separate us from the love of God in Christ Jesus our Lord" (*Romans 8:37–39*).

"The kingdom of the world has become the kingdom of our Lord and of his Christ, and he shall reign for ever and ever" (*Revelation 11:15*).

THE APOSTLES' CREED

I believe in God the Father Almighty, Maker of heaven and earth.

And in Jesus Christ, his only Son, our Lord, who was conceived by the Holy Spirit, born of the Virgin Mary, suffered under Pontius Pilate, was crucified, dead and buried. He descended into hades. The third day he rose again from the dead. He ascended into heaven, and sitteth on the right hand of God, the Father Almighty. From thence he shall come to judge the quick and the dead.

I believe in the Holy Spirit, the holy Christian church, the communion of saints, the forgiveness of sins, the resurrection of the body, and the life everlasting. Amen.

LUTHER'S EXPLANATION OF THE APOSTLES' CREED

I believe in God the Father almighty, Maker of heaven and earth.

What does this mean?

I believe that God has created me and all that exists. He has given me and still preserves my body and soul with all their powers.

He provides me with food and clothing, home and family, daily work, and all I need from day to day. God also protects me in time of danger and guards me from every evil.

All this he does out of fatherly and divine goodness and mercy, though I do not deserve it.

Therefore I surely ought to thank and praise, serve and obey him.

This is most certainly true.

I believe in Jesus Christ his only Son, our Lord; who was conceived by the Holy Spirit, born of the Virgin Mary; suffered under Pontius Pilate, was crucified, dead, and buried; he descended into hades; the third day he rose again from the dead; he ascended into heaven, and sitteth on the right hand of God the Father almighty; from thence he shall come to judge the quick and the dead.

What does this mean?

I believe that Jesus Christ—true God, Son of the Father from eternity, and true man, born of the Virgin Mary—is my Lord.

He has redeemed me, a lost and condemned person, saved me at great cost from sin, death, and the power of the devil—not with silver or gold, but with his holy and precious suffering and death.

All this he has done that I may be his own, live under him in his kingdom, and serve him in everlasting righteousness, innocence, and blessedness, just as he is risen from the dead and lives and rules eternally.

This is most certainly true.

I believe in the Holy Spirit; the holy Christian church, the communion of saints; the forgiveness of sins; the resurrection of the body; and the life everlasting. Amen.

What does this mean?

I believe that I cannot by my own understanding or effort believe in Jesus Christ my Lord, or come to him. But the Holy Spirit has called me through the gospel, enlightened me with his gifts, and sanctified and kept me in true faith.

In the same way he calls, gathers, enlightens, and sanctifies the whole Christian church on earth, and keeps it united with Jesus Christ in the one true faith.

In this Christian church day after day he fully forgives my sins and the sins of all believers.

On the last day he will raise me and all the dead and give me and all believers in Christ eternal life.

This is most certainly true.

THE CATECHISM

What is the highest and most important knowledge?

The highest and most important knowledge is to know God and his son, Jesus Christ.

"And this is eternal life, that they know thee the only true God, and Jesus Christ whom thou hast sent" (*John 17:3*).

What is the church?

The church is the whole company of those who, confessing Jesus Christ as Savior and Lord, are united in fellowship with God and with one another.

"So then you are no longer strangers and sojourners, but you are fellow citizens with the saints and members of the household of God, built upon the foundation of the apostles and prophets, Christ Jesus himself being the cornerstone" (*Ephesians 2:19, 20*).

Who is the Holy Spirit?

The Holy Spirit is God everywhere present and powerful, working in us, in the church, and in the world.

"Now to him who by the power at work within us is able to do far more abundantly than all that we ask or think, to him be glory in the church and in Christ Jesus to all generations, for ever and ever. Amen" (*Ephesians 3:20, 21*).

What is conversion?

Conversion is that act by which man turns with repentance and faith from sin to God.

"The time is fulfilled, and the kingdom of God is at hand; repent, and believe in the gospel" (*Mark 1:15*).

What is the gospel?

The gospel is the good news of God's redeeming love for man, made known in the life, death, and resurrection of Jesus Christ and his continuing rule over us.

"For God so loved the world that he gave his only Son, that whoever believes in him should not perish but have eternal life. For God sent the Son into the world, not to condemn the world, but that the world might be saved through him" (*John 3:16, 17*).

What is the purpose of the church?

The purpose of the church is to celebrate new life in Christ, build up one another in the Christian faith, proclaim the gospel to all men, and be his servants in the world. These are the duties of the members of a church.

"You are a chosen race, a royal priesthood, a holy nation, God's own people, that you may declare the wonderful deeds of him who called you out of darkness into his marvelous light. Once you were no people but now you are God's people; once you had not received mercy but now you have received mercy" (*1 Peter 2:9, 10*).

What is the source of the church's life?

The life of the church has its source in God. It is created and renewed by his Spirit and Word, the holy sacraments, and prayer.

"There is one body and one Spirit, just as you were called to the one hope that belongs to your call, one Lord, one faith, one baptism, one God and Father of us all, who is above all and through all and in all" (*Ephesians 4:4–6*).

Who is God?

God is personal, eternal Spirit, Father of our Lord Jesus Christ, and our Father.

"For from him and through him and to him are all things. To him be glory for ever. Amen." (*Romans 11:36*).

What does it mean to be a man?

To be a man is to be created in the likeness of God, free and responsible in relation to God, the world, neighbor, and self.

"Thou hast made him little less than God, and dost crown him with glory and honor. Thou hast given him dominion over the works of thy hands; thou hast put all things under his feet" (*Psalm 8:5, 6*).

What do we believe about the Bible?

We believe in the Holy Scriptures, the Old and New Testaments, as the Word of God and the only perfect rule for faith, doctrine, and conduct.

"No prophecy ever came by the impulse of man, but men moved by the Holy Spirit spoke from God" (*2 Peter 1:21*).

How is the Word of God to be used?

The Word of God is rightly used when guided by the Holy Spirit we lay hold of its truth, treasure it in our hearts, and practice it in our lives.

"Do your best to present yourself to God as one approved, a workman who has no need to be ashamed, rightly handling the word of truth" (*2 Timothy 2:15*).

How does God make himself known?

God makes himself known in the works of creation, the events of history, and the voice of conscience, but supremely in Jesus Christ as revealed in Holy Scripture.

"For he has made known to us in all wisdom and insight the mystery of his will, according to his purpose which he set forth in Christ as a plan for the fullness of time, to unite all things in him, things in heaven and things on earth" (*Ephesians 1:9, 10*).

What is God's relationship to man and the world?

God calls the world into being by his Word, upholds it by his power, creates man in his own likeness, and cares for all things according to his wisdom.

"He is before all things, and in him all things hold together" (*Colossians 1:17*).

Who is Jesus?

Jesus of Nazareth is God's Son, our Savior and Lord, who according to God's promise came into the world to save sinners.

"The saying is sure and worthy of full acceptance, that Christ Jesus came into the world to save sinners. And I am the foremost of sinners" (*1 Timothy 1:15*).

What was the highest expression of the Savior's love for man?

The highest expression of the Savior's love for man was his suffering and death on the cross for the sins of man.

"In this is love, not that we loved God but that he loved us and sent his Son to be the expiation for our sins" (*1 John 4:10*).

What is the significance of Jesus' suffering and death?

By his suffering and death, Jesus has conquered sin, death, and the power of the devil and has made fellowship with God possible for us.

"There is therefore now no condemnation for those who are in Christ Jesus. For the law of the Spirit of life in Christ Jesus has set me free from the law of sin and death" (*Romans 8:1, 2*).

What is sin?

Sin is our willful refusal or failure to love God, his creation, and our neighbor as ourselves.

"This is the message we have heard from him and proclaim to you, that God is light and in him is no darkness at all. If we say we have fellowship with him while we walk in darkness, we lie and do not live acording to the truth" (*1 John 1:5, 6*).

What are the results of sin?

The results of sin are that we hurt others and ourselves, weaken our ability to know and do God's will, and, above all, separate ourselves from him.

"Do not be deceived; God is not mocked, for whatever a man sows, that he will also reap" (*Galatians 6:7*).

What does it mean to believe in the Trinity?

To believe in the Trinity is to confess that God is one, and that he continually and personally makes himself known to us as Father, Son, and Holy Spirit.

"The grace of the Lord Jesus Christ and the love of God and the fellowship of the Holy Spirit be with you all" (*2 Corinthians 13:14*).

What is the significance of Jesus' resurrection?

The resurrection of Jesus Christ from the dead is the assurance that he is Lord of life and death, and the first fruits of a new creation.

"But thanks be to God, who gives us the victory through our Lord Jesus Christ" (*1 Corinthians 15:57*).

What is justification?

Justification is an act of God in Christ by which he forgives us our sins and accepts us as righteous.

"Therefore, since we are justified by faith, we have peace with God through our Lord Jesus Christ" (*Romans 1:5*).

What is sanctification?

Sanctification is that work of the Holy Spirit by which he cleanses us from sin and enables us to live a new life according to Christ's example.

"Let not sin therefore reign in your mortal bodies, to make you obey their passions. Do not yield your members to sin as instruments of wickedness, but yield yourselves to God as men who have been brought from death to life, and your members to God as instruments of righteousness" (*Romans 6:12, 13*).

What is a sacrament?

A sacrament is a visible and outward sign of an invisible and spiritual grace. The sacraments commanded by Jesus Christ are baptism and the Lord's Supper.

"So those who received his word were baptized, and there were added that day about three thousand souls. And they devoted themselves to the apostles' teaching and fellowship, to the breaking of bread and the prayers" (*Acts 2:41, 42*).

What is baptism?

Baptism is the sacred use of water which was commanded by Jesus Christ to signify God's cleansing of our sins and our consecration to God.

"Go therefore and make disciples of all nations, baptizing them in the name of the Father and of the Son and of the Holy Spirit, teaching them to observe all that I have commanded you; and lo, I am with you always, to the close of the age" (*Matthew 28:19, 20*).

What is the Lord's Supper?

The Lord's Supper is the sacred use of bread and the cup which was commanded by Jesus Christ, by which we remember his suffering for us, proclaim his death until he comes, and in communion with one another partake of him in faith.

"For I received from the Lord what I also delivered to you, that the Lord Jesus on the night when he was betrayed took bread, and when he had given thanks, he broke it, and said, 'This is my body which is broken for you. Do this in remembrance of me.' In the same way also the cup after supper, saying, 'This cup is the new covenant in my blood. Do this, as often as you drink it, in remembrance of me.' For as often as you eat this bread and drink the cup, you proclaim the Lord's death until he comes" (*1 Corinthians 11:23–26*).

What is prayer?

Prayer is speaking and listening to God, lifting up our hearts to him in adoration and thanksgiving, confessing our sins, seeking his help for ourselves and others, and waiting expectantly on him.

"Truly, truly, I say to you, if you ask anything of the Father, he will give it to you in my name. Hitherto you have asked nothing in my name; ask, and you will receive, that your joy may be full" (*John 16:23, 24*).

What is the meaning of death?

Death means that our earthly life will come to an end and that we must all give an account of our lives before the judgment seat of Christ.

"For we must all appear before the judgment seat of Christ, so that each one may receive good or evil, according to what he has done in the body" (*2 Corinthians 5:10*).

What does the Bible teach about the final judgment?

The Bible teaches, concerning the final judgment, that Christ as king and judge shall separate the righteous from the unrighteous. The righteous will live forever with God and his people, and the unrighteous will be separated forever from the presence of God.

"Do not marvel at this; for the hour is coming when all who are in the tombs will hear his voice and come forth, those who have done good, to the resurrection of life, and those who have done evil, to the resurrection of judgment" (*John 5:28, 29*).

What is the Christian hope?

The Christian hope is the assurance that God's purposes for his pilgrim people will end in triumph at the return of Christ, that we shall be raised with him, and that the Lord will reign forever with his church in the age to come.

"In all these things we are more than conquerors through him who loved us. For I am sure that neither death, nor life, nor angels, nor principalities, nor things present, nor things to come, nor powers, nor height, nor depth, nor anything else in all creation, will be able to separate us from the love of God in Christ Jesus our Lord" (*Romans 8:37–39*).

"The kingdom of the world has become the kingdom of our Lord and of his Christ, and he shall reign for ever and ever" (*Revelation 11:15*).

Notes

Notes

Notes

Notes

Notes

Notes

Notes

Notes

Notes